MASTER Working from Home Successfully

More than 100 Must know tips for every person working from home

Garry Bryant

from various sources. Please consult a licensed professional before attempting any techniques outlined in this book.

By reading this document, the reader agrees that under no circumstances is the author responsible for any losses, direct or indirect, that are incurred as a result of the use of the information contained within this document, including, but not limited to, errors, omissions, or inaccuracies.

Table of Contents

Introduction

Having worked suited and booted in a typical 9 to 5 office environment for more than 12 years, I was offered the unique opportunity to work remotely from home. One of the main deciding factors in coming to this major decision in my career was that I'd already missed out on so many 'firsts' that I would simply never be able to get back again. As a father of two, the early years of development were important to me, and I soon realized that, with all the things I was missing out on, my work / home-life balance was totally out of whack. Something needed to be done about it and sooner rather than later.

First swimming lessons, first recitals and plays - each of these represented precious time and experiences that could never be replaced again. Time is finite and no one wants to waste even one second that could be spent doing things that are worthwhile. It's more important to contribute to the growth and development of family ties, rather than being stuck in endless meetings while trying to climb the corporate ladder.

It took me 12 years to figure out exactly what I was sacrificing and losing out on! Fortunately, 5 years ago I was offered an opportunity to begin balancing my work and home life by relocating my office to my home. This book is a result of everything I have learned, experienced and discovered for myself through trial and error over the last five years; it will assist you by providing you with more than 100 Tips and Techniques that everyone working from a home based office should know of. Naturally these tips and techniques didn't fall into my lap by accident, instead, they have been gathered on the basis of trial and error. Learning and growing as I've gone along; I've learned to get the balance between home and family right and put those things that matter in perspective.

The book answers questions such as:

- How can I get more work done?
- How can I separate work from home life?
- How can I make sure I'm not forgotten by my colleagues?
- How can I prove myself to my colleagues from home?
- How can I have a better working from home routine?

The following pages will provide you with a wealth of information that you can begin to implement and make part of your daily routine immediately. While it can take some time to nail these habits and routines down, they will make creating a more harmonious balance between your work and home-life not only achievable, but something to look forward to.

As you learn and begin to implement some of these ideas into your own life, you'll see that time is much more valuable than money and not having to commute to an office can make a huge difference to your life. When you think about it, no more commute means less stress and less time wasted in traffic, time you can use to do something worthwhile, and spend more quality time with family.

Chapter 1:

Why am I Working from

Home?

One of the very first things that you need to clarify within your own mind is your main motivation for wanting to work from home. This could be for a diverse number of reasons. You may be there due to a medical crisis that simply cannot be averted at this time. This could lead to a limited period where you're working from home while you recover, for example after major surgery.

Some individuals are completely anti-social, and it makes sense to be isolated from the world, communicating via technology, where they can hide behind computers and cameras, faxes and other means of communication where they can remove the social component from the equation. These individuals could be anyone, from introverts to those suffering from PTSD or other emotional illnesses. They may operate under pen names rather than their own, and hide behind the safety of a computer, rather than having to face the world and deal with people. Many of these individuals operate their own businesses effectively, as long as they get to remain indoors and away from the regular hustle and bustle of the world.

For others, choosing to work from home is out of curiosity, and the need to prove to themselves and others that they have what it takes to be self-disciplined enough to make a go of it.

What I can tell you though before you dive right into making this life-changing decision is that you need to consider several factors. Some of these might include:

Saving Time and Money - Commuting

Saving both time and money from your daily commute each day—we have all experienced the frustration and boredom of getting stuck in rush hour bumper-to-bumper traffic, unproductive time that you can never get back. Even making use of a hands-free communication device and trying to make business calls is not always successful while commuting.

For many that have a long commute to the office, trying to avoid the daily rush of traffic means leaving home several hours before the rush begins. While this could prove to be productive as you'd be getting into the office way earlier than your colleagues, it can also place a lot more pressure on family relationships, because family hardly gets to see you. In the end, something's got to give. Only you can decide whether the sacrifice you're currently making is worthwhile in the long run.

Photo Credit 4657743 from Pixabay

Prove Them Wrong!

If you're as lucky as I was, where a business opportunity was presented to me to work from home, and you're able to pull it off, grab it with both hands and hold on tight because it's likely to be one hell of a ride! This could well be your very own golden ticket to success: it doesn't come along every day, and you need to be sure that you're not only up to it, but that you're going to put your very best foot forward to make it work for both you and the employer who entrusted you with this opportunity.

Some organizations agree to allow their employees to work remotely, only to be able to find reasons to terminate employment down the line. Not everyone is cut out to be able to work on their own, unsupervised. It requires drive, determination and tenacity, as well as being self-disciplined enough to get up and work each and every day, rather than finding excuses for why things haven't been done.

Weigh up the Pros and Cons

For me personally, there are more pros than cons to working from a home office, and while it may take some initial trial and error and getting used to, the sacrifice and learning curve that you have to go through will definitely be worthwhile in the long-run. This is my main reason for piecing this work together: these have been my own personal experiences that I've had to endure. Some of them have been amazing and highlights of my work career, while others have taken me on some very steep learning curves. I'd like to share this knowledge with you so that you're able to learn from the good and discard the bad, or at least be forewarned and prepared before taking the leap!

Things I Wish I Had Known

Many of these tips and techniques are things that I wish that I had known before starting out on my home office journey, as they would have saved me from being knocked back a peg or two on a number of occasions. On the other hand, had I not had to experience each of these things personally, I may have remained stagnant in my career without being offered a number of valuable opportunities to move up the corporate ladder and prove my worth to my employers, on my own, without having someone looking over my shoulder day in and day out.

This is Your Journey

I genuinely owe my success to the victories and losses experienced on my own journey. I hope that they will benefit you in the same way. As a word of encouragement right from the outset, some situations and advice may not be applicable to you due to the nature of your industry. I had to make these things my very own, and I'd encourage you to do the same. Sift through each tidbit and absorb the ideas, tips and techniques that will work best for your situation. It's the only way to be able to move forward and cement yourself as indispensable to the organization you're working with.

As with all advice, take whatever works for you, and leave the rest. There are a number of techniques and tools that you can implement to make your life easier.

Chapter 2:

The Ideal Work

Environment

One of the first things to get nailed down correctly before diving into working from home is creating the ideal work environment. The area that you're going to work from needs to be set up correctly, just like an office, in order for you to not only feel like you're getting the job done, but also that it's a professional space. The following are some considerations that should be made when choosing the ideal office set up in your home.

Comfort and Ergonomics

Your setup needs to include a good, ergonomically correct chair that offers sufficient support, as you're going to need to sit on it for an extended amount of time each day. A cheap office chair or dining room chair simply won't do. Make sure that the chair provides you with sufficient lumbar support, while still being comfortable. You also don't want to look at a chair that's cheap all day. The price tag is usually in proportion to the amount of wear you're likely to get out of it. You want something that's robust, comfortable, and will stand the test of time. If you suffer from back problems, this is something that you're going to need to address when you go shopping for the ideal office chair. It should support your back and alleviate pressure, rather than adding to it.

Next comes a good desk, with sufficient space for you to work on. Depending on what you do for a living, having enough space to do it on is right up there with choosing the right chair. Avoid sharing the desk with someone else in the family - this doesn't make your 'home office' yours, it's also then bound to become a dumping ground for things unrelated to your work, which will cause chaos and disorder. These are two things that you want to avoid at all costs.

Internet Connectivity

Make sure that you have excellent high-speed internet connectivity. You're going to need this for both video conferencing and file sharing. Choose to go with cloud file storage as this will free up space on whatever device you're using, but also will also protect your documents and information, should anything happen to your physical hardware. Choose fiber over older types of connections, as it's more reliable and faster than conventional, older connectivity.

Focus on speed, reliability and minimize throttling or tethering on the line, as this could prove to be frustrating when it comes to working internationally where video images either freeze out on you or pixelate because your internet speed is not up to scratch.

VOIP

Another solid piece of advice I can offer is to try and use VOIP (Voice over Internet Protocol) and keep a separate business number from your home number. Because I report to a company in the United States, I have a US number in the United Kingdom, where I'm based. This works perfectly for clients, colleagues and associates who communicate with me as if I were in the USA.

If you happen to be working for yourself, dealing with international clients (or an extensive client database), this solution is one that you should seriously consider as it has so many more benefits than conventional telephony.

The single most important benefit to choosing the VOIP option is cost saving. While conventional telephony charges per minute or unit base, VOIP is billed on a monthly basis, regardless of usage. When you're in a similar situation to what I am, working remotely between two different countries and relying heavily on teleconferencing and video calls, this is the very best solution possible.

It's also generally cloud-based, and is more reliable than landlines provided by service providers who may be regulated by bandwidth constrictions. VOIP makes use of bandwidth in another way, packaging data together. Other benefits are that it's compatible with both hardware and software that you already have, and you don't need to invest in anything particularly sophisticated to make the switch.

Dedicated Work Space - Don't Share!

Find a suitable space in your home that you can dedicate specifically to work. This should ideally be another room where you can shut yourself off during your work hours and remain undisturbed from other outside noise, disruption and interference. The ideal space should have a door that can be closed while you are working. This is especially important when it comes to handling tele-conferencing or video-conferencing calls. If this is a large part of your business dealings with others, it may be a good idea to invest in a high quality headset that will not only drown out unnecessary background noise, but will help you focus on your calls.

Sharing a space with another member of the family can be disruptive and could easily lead to procrastination. You could be tempted to fall into the trap of chatting about all sorts of things rather than actually doing your work. It's also difficult to establish firm boundaries in this situation. When you have your own dedicated space, it's easier to close the door when you're working, or even place a 'Do not disturb' sign on the door when you're in the middle of a conference call, or you're working towards meeting a tight deadline. Boundaries are healthy when it comes to your home office.

Photo Credit - Erika Wittlieb from Pixabay

Business Tools

Make sure that you have all the right business tools necessary to run your business at your disposal and within reach. This could include anything from pens to paper clips, a stapler, ruler, planner and even Post-it notes if necessary. Everything should be neatly organized and within reach, so you don't waste precious time looking for business tools that should be readily available.

Depending on what is required of you, you may need a whiteboard with markers, a flipboard with paper to make notes on and other larger value items that will make running a business from your home not only viable, but successful.

If you're only just starting out and want to keep your costs to a minimum, draw up a lean list that you can add to as you go along. Your lean list should include things you simply cannot do without, and require for your business to be able function effectively.

Some items on this list would include a desk, chair, laptop or desktop computer, relevant software and basic stationery items to get started.

Light and Ventilation

Some other key considerations when setting up your workspace should be ensuring that the designated area has excellent ventilation as this increases productivity. If you've decided to set up in a basement or another room where windows don't or can't open, it's strongly advised that ventilation units such as extraction fans and thermostatically controlled air-conditioning units are installed and maintained regularly. If the room has insufficient airflow, you could easily feel drowsy and unable to concentrate on what needs to be done. Your level of concentration needs to remain at its peak as far as possible.

Natural light is another contributing factor to creating the best possible work area. While mentioning windows above, one of the problems with windows that open, facing gardens could potentially be a noise hazard, especially if you happen to own dogs that enjoy barking. As far as you possibly can, choose your office room carefully while considering each of the factors listed in this chapter, without compromising on efficacy.

Confidential Information /
Intellectual Property

Depending on the type of work you do, you may need additional tools such as printers, scanners, shredders, and filing cabinets that can be locked. This is not necessarily to say that someone in your family is likely to commit espionage, but you have been given a mandate by the company that you represent to make sure their Intellectual Property (IP) is kept as safe as possible. The last thing you need is to go to the kitchen for a cup of coffee and return to find your 5-year old drawing all over a contract you need to deliver in 20 minutes!

Consider each possible scenario that could potentially happen in your home office and implement security measures to counteract and prevent these things from happening. If you have small children who love to be around you while you're working, set something up where they have their own 'tools' and possibly even a small desk and chair that's separate from your own work. Make sure that they understand the boundaries between their own things and yours. If you need to leave your office for any reason, make sure that they aren't left unsupervised. The best thing to do would be to guide them out of the office and close or lock the door until you return.

Be realistic about the value of your company's intellectual property or confidential information. They have entrusted you with this information, be sure that you are worthy of this trust and put safeguards in place that prevent any of this information from falling into the wrong hands, even if it is your beloved 5-year old's!

Chapter 3:

Computer Software

Probably one of the biggest challenges that companies need to get right when their employees work remotely is technology. This doesn't need to be as challenging as what it was a few short years ago though. While it used to be necessary to purchase expensive software packages, paying exorbitant license fees outright, most software these days is offered on a subscription basis, making it way more affordable for those working on their own.

Software / Freeware and Licensing

Spending a bit of time online can provide you with a number of freeware options that can help jumpstart your remote business. Google offers Google Docs free for personal use and for business G Suite, which has document editing, cloud storage, collaboration tools, calendars and Gmail, starting at around $6 per month. This could prove perfect when saving to the cloud or sharing files with others remotely. Another well-known branded product, Microsoft Office 365, is currently only around US $10.00 per month with similar tools. There are often substantial discounts available by paying for a 12-month package up front.

Depending on the operating system you're using, there are many free apps available via Apple or Google Play store. These apps can do anything from assist with productivity when working in groups of people (Microsoft Teams), to sharing files (Google docs). Other cloud-based software is specifically designed to support and encourage teamwork and collaboration.

Search for applications that will help you manage your day more productively and assist you to get more things done, rather than distracting you. The last thing you need is to have software running that doesn't serve a specific purpose - making your life easier! When deciding on software for your work at home operation, make sure that you are using all the features of the software. A sound example of this is Microsoft Outlook: use its full capacity to manage your day using the calendar, scheduling and meeting management functions. Alerts can be set for important calls or tasks that need to be managed. Another well-known branded product like Microsoft Office 365 is currently only around US $10.00 per month with similar tools. There are often substantial discounts available by paying for a 12-month package up front.

Virus Protection Software

Be wary of simply downloading applications for fun—
you need to ensure that they're always from a reliable
source. Do some homework to make sure that what
you're getting is going to do what it promises to do.
Unnecessary software is going to take up space and
slow your system down. Carefully consider your needs
before adding anything new, and only add programs
that you are actually going to make use of.

An important consideration when working with loads
of correspondence is that some of it is SPAM, and your
system can run the risk of being infected with computer
viruses. Choose a reliable antivirus software, even if you
need to pay for it on a monthly basis or annually. It's
better than losing all your information or risking any of
the company's information becoming corrupt because
your system isn't sufficiently protected.

Photo Credit - Gerd Altmann from Pixabay

Rely on Company IT Products

If you're like me, working remotely for another organization, let their IT division direct you when it comes to the software requirements necessary for your job. They may have specific parameters and protocols in place to protect their intellectual property on the internet. Allow them remote access to your system whenever necessary and communicate with them immediately especially if you feel that there's possibly been a security breach.

Many large corporations make use of specialist programs, or even systems and programs that have been designed especially for them. Make use of these rather than stepping outside the guidelines: there are reasons why these systems are in place.

Unfortunately we live in a day and age where it's easy for hackers to get into your system. Large corporations invest a lot of money to ensure that their information is protected; when working remotely, follow their advice as far as technology is concerned.

Report Security Breaches Immediately

If you suspect that there's been a breach with any security protocols, or that you have a virus on your system, report this to your supervisor or IT Division immediately. Don't try and correct the issue on your own. Sometimes these viruses have multiple layers and when you don't know exactly what you're doing, your good intentions could lead to more harm than good.

If you're on a network, this could be potentially dangerous to others on the same network as well.

Be Sensible

Use both common sense and sound business judgement when it comes to choosing computer software: rather be safe than sorry! It's better to pay for tried, tested and reputable software, rather than settling on computer applications that are available to all but have little to no credibility in the market.

Chapter 4:

Expenses, Costs and

Utilities

This is normally an area where large corporations score by having employees work remotely. There's a whole list of savings to their bottom-line business expenditure that you're now possibly picking up for them. When you think about it, you're now paying the bill for the internet connection, power and other utilities. Some of these costs may not even be that obvious to you; things like tea, coffee, toilet paper and even that bagel you had for breakfast this morning that would normally have been supplied!

Freelance Expenses

These necessary costs can be approached in several ways—if you're working as a freelance, make a list of everything you use to keep your business running. This could be anything from those things mentioned above, to paper, envelopes, other stationery, printers, ink refills, furniture (that you've had to supply), and the space you occupy to run your business daily. Believe it or not, you can also include a portion of your common areas, such as the kitchen and bathroom, and even the living room, if you have meetings in your home.

Remember to include a percentage of your utility costs, such as water, lights, property taxes and even refuse removal. Expense everything that can be offset as running costs of your business.

This may depend on your location, but your motor vehicle, your fuel, the wear and tear on your vehicle, your cell phone. Insurance costs for anything that is business related. Capture all of this information so that it can be submitted as part of your annual tax return. You may be pleasantly surprised by just how much you are able to claim.

When it comes to your motor vehicle and all related costs, you will need to keep accurate records including a logbook, mileage to and from meetings, as well as personal travel. Without this information, your claim won't be processed to include travel. Tax laws vary by country, so it's worthwhile either hiring a tax consultant or investigating this further yourself to find out what you are entitled to claim for as a potential rebate.

Employee Expenses

When working as an employee these lines can become a bit blurred if not specified and agreed to up front. In many instances, the employer is prepared to pick up these costs and there's no need to panic about being out of pocket at the end of each month with huge utility bills. Remember that you are physically employed by them to provide a service. If you were working from their offices, they would need to provide you with all tools necessary for you to perform your job to the very best of your ability, so it's common sense that there be a mutual agreement in place regarding costs. In addition to this, if there's a written agreement in place, make sure that there's room for it to be reviewed on a regular basis, as costs can change and the last thing you need is to foot the bill yourself by supporting your employer's business undertaking.

Accurate records should be maintained and updated on a regular basis for all expenses that you pay for out of pocket. This is to ensure that you can submit these claims to your employer on a regular basis. Most companies have a reimbursement plan in place. Whether they have a specific form that needs to be filled out and submitted to your supervisor or to the payroll department, they will have a way to repay you for any money that you have spent on their behalf.

Another way in which organizations support their employees is by providing them with company business credit cards. This is usually attached to the department that you represent, and cost codes will automatically be processed by the finance department on your behalf. In the event that you do have this type of benefit available to you, it's in your best interest to only use it for business and remain totally honest in your dealings with the company. This is yet another way to prove both loyalty and integrity to the organization you're working for.

Tax Breaks – Check into Tax Relief

If you're freelancing, many of these costs can be offset, and depending on where in the world you are, you may be entitled to a certain percentage of all operating expenditure incurred back as tax relief. Keep accurate records of all of your expenses so that you can submit these along with your tax documents annually. If you're not sure how to go about submitting these costs, or exactly what you're entitled to claim back, it could be helpful to consult with a tax practitioner or advisor who can guide you through the process. In certain instances, the actual tax office themselves may be able to walk you through this process.

Chapter 5:

If Something Hits the Fan!

Being Prepared

How prepared are you should something hit the fan? While this is normally the furthest thing from our minds when working remotely, it needs to be considered. Unfortunately we live in a world that is becoming more and more violent and crime is on the increase globally. Are you covered in the event of a burglary? Some of the ways to pre-empt losing everything is by encrypting your device drives through systems like Nordlocker, LastPass and Bitlocker. Each of these can be funded monthly, making it less painful than having to face a large upfront payment for coverage. By choosing one of these three options, at least none of your data will be compromised, even if you happen to lose all your hardware.

Protect Your Data

Another sound piece of advice when it comes to your work stored on your computer / laptop or tablet: make regular backup copies onto external drives that can be safely stored and secured away. By doing so, you'll never face having to recapture years or even decades of information. The key to this being successful is to keep this portable external drive in a different location from your other hardware. The last thing you need is to lose it all simultaneously.

Are You Sufficiently Covered?

When it comes to physical insurance, it's important to make sure that you are covered for the physical equipment that you have in your home at any given time. In many instances, insurance agencies are prepared to cover something under 'Administration,' but they shy away from covering hardware, as these are usually high value items and naturally, this is where insurance companies stand to lose the most.

Where possible make sure that ALL your equipment is covered on your insurance policy, even if it falls under the 'all risks' section. You may need to jump through a few hoops to get everything insured, as insurance companies are becoming more tech-savvy themselves, often requesting Serial Numbers of everything, or cash slips to provide 'proof of purchase' or 'proof of ownership' – I've always found that the best way to deal with this is to take physical photographs of each item, along with the serial numbers, and submit everything along with purchase prices as well as projected replacement values. The more information you're able to provide them with, the more likely they're able to get back to you with a good deal.

Make sure that your equipment is insured for replacement value of equal or better. As we all know, items depreciate in value over time. You need to protect these assets as they essentially 'are' your business. Rather pay a few extra dollars each month to make sure that you receive enough of a payout in the event of something going wrong, than finding out the hard way!

It's Not My Equipment!

If the equipment you're working with belongs to your employer, it makes sound business sense to double check that the equipment is covered by insurance while in your care, and that you have no liability should anything happen to it, such as a burglary. Don't be naïve and think that because you've been given a laptop and a cellphone to use for business purposes, they're automatically insured by the business. You could be in for a very rude awakening. Rather be safe than sorry and get all the facts. Make sure that things like laptops and cell phones are also covered under an 'out and about' clause for whenever you're travelling, or have these items on you while attending meetings.

Other Legal Liability and Insurance

Some final considerations regarding insurance include legal liability for when a colleague or customer is visiting your home for work purposes. Should someone slip and fall or injure themselves, are you sufficiently covered financially and in line with the law in the country that you're operating in? What is your risk or liability? You need to reduce your own liability as far as possible. This may mean physically opening up your home for a legal broker or insurance firm to assess the level of risk. While you may see this as intrusive, if it's going to protect you in the long run, it's worth allowing them into your home to inspect the property. You never know, they may even be able to point out certain flaws or weak areas that can be corrected with a little effort from your side.

Motor Vehicle Insurance

If you're freelancing, ensure that your motor vehicle is covered for business purposes, as this type of insurance could potentially be different from normal automotive insurance. Make sure that you're in possession of all the facts so that you're not surprised when something happens. Whether it's coverage for collision or for theft, fire or vandalism, having sound and sufficient vehicle insurance is highly recommended.

Shop Around

If the insurance has been left to you to finalize, don't settle for the first price quoted—it's worthwhile getting comparative quotes as your age, environment and living situation could all influence the overall costs quoted by the insurance agency. Look for an insurance broker that's able to provide you with a variety of options, or there are a number of services online that offer numerous quotes simultaneously without trying to strong-arm you into signing up with any particular service provider.

In this instance, you may find that one company offers a better deal on motor vehicle insurance, while another offers a cost saving on your physical assets or office equipment. There's nothing stopping you from going with multiple service providers in order to secure the best price possible.

Chapter 6:

Make Lists

Prioritize Where Possible

Learn to prioritize important tasks each day by making lists and using tracking tools. These help you become more organized, focused, and identify what needs to be completed on a daily basis in order of importance. It's not only an important tool to plan and schedule your day, but it can also help you tackle each task that needs to be done daily (even those that seem to be unimportant and mundane).

Figuring out what's important may require some guidance from management, mentors or supervisors initially. If you are working on certain projects as part of a team, take direction from whoever is most senior on the project but whatever you do, make sure that you're not the one that drops the ball!

Tools for Lists

I've been using Evernote for more than 7 years: it allows me to search through notes and lists and go over old tasks and projects. This app also helps me create a master list that I can present to my boss on a weekly basis, allowing them to see exactly what's going on. Even though it's just bullet points showing upcoming tasks, completed tasks, concerns and important wins, it helps me remain focused on what needs to be accomplished every single day.

Similar apps available are OneNote and Trello. Before going ahead and settling for an app to keep all your tasks in one place, make sure the app is reliable, has support and is not likely to be discontinued in the future. This is easy enough to do by performing some research on Google. The last thing that you need to be doing is capturing all of your data, projects and information on an app that's about to expire: the point of going with an app in the first place is to streamline your productivity, rather than set it back. Do some homework before jumping in feet first!

To Do Lists

You may prefer going the good old fashioned manual route, setting out a physical 'To Do List' that allows you to write down and capture everything that needs doing. A physical 'To Do List' can prove to be extremely effective as it's more visual than an app on your phone could be. With a physical list, you can look at the BIG picture of everything that needs to be done during the course of a day. You can then decide what needs to take precedence and what's most important.

Some individuals prefer to go the route of least resistance and choose to get the smaller stuff out of the way, allowing them more time to devote on what is more important after. Whatever way is comfortable for you, do your best to work through each 'To Do List' daily.

You may even want to capture the most important things that need doing on a flipchart or whiteboard that's close by and easily accessible. As you've managed to complete each task, mark them off or erase them from your whiteboard. You may just find that as you begin doing one thing, it leads to other sub-tasks being broken down further into more manageable bits. In this event, add each of these items to your 'To Do List' and work through them one by one.

Assess Your Day

Get into the habit of setting aside some quiet time at the end of the day to consider what you've managed to accomplish, what you should've accomplished, and what you still need to accomplish. Items accomplished should be physically crossed off as this provides a psychological way for you to recognize that there's progress being made. It also allows you to re-prioritize items that should be rearranged on your 'To Do List' as they happen.

Making and sticking to lists creates efficient and effective work habits; it also keeps us motivated towards doing the things we need to do on a daily basis. Some of these tasks may be routine and repetitive, but that's what the work life is all about - it's getting those smaller things out of the way to make place for what is more impactful and important.

Evening Analysis

For some, it's effective to spend 10 minutes at nighttime, contemplating the day and what has been accomplished, and then writing down the top 5 things that MUST be achieved the following day. The reason for this process is that your subconscious will have time to process each of the tasks while you are sleeping, and by the morning you will have a clear head and clear direction as to what you need to do to complete the tasks at hand.

Whichever option of List Making you decide to settle for, make sure that it works for you. Some companies have their own activity tracking systems in place, in which case you may need to follow these in-house procedures and protocols.

Chapter 7:

Effective Time

Management

Probably one of the most challenging things to master when you're working from your own home-based office is managing your time effectively. It's easy to become distracted by the external noise of everyday life that constantly surrounds us. In this chapter, we're going to look at some of the things to consider so that you can maximize every moment spent working, rather than allowing the sands of time to slip through your fingers, never to be retrieved again.

All Time Has an Expiration Date

We've already mentioned that time is finite and you can never get it back again. If you allow yourself to become distracted by even the smallest, insignificant things, when you're meant to be doing something productive, it can take a while to play 'catch-up.' There's nothing to be done once a deadline has expired and you're late in handing in a proposal, quotation, report, or any number of other things that may be required for a project to move forward.

There's a reason for things having deadlines attached to them, figuring out why this is important and then doing whatever it takes shows those who are depending on you that you take your role within their organization as seriously as they do. It also proves that you can be trusted to work remotely in the first place, and that you're not short-changing them when it comes to your time.

Write Down Everything That Needs Doing

This could be done via a 'To Do List' as discussed in the previous chapter, or you can add each item to a productivity app like Trello, where you can easily manage your tasks, dragging and dropping things effortlessly from things to do, to being processed, to complete. Some of these apps allow you to include teammates and others who are associated with the same project, so that everyone is onboard with exactly what's happening with scheduled tasks. As each task is complete, mark it off your list as 'done.'

There's a psychological reason for physically writing things down. Once you've written it down, it's actually out of your head. Aim to get things down on paper, on your app or on your whiteboard. It will physically make room for you to concentrate on other things that are maybe just as important.

Focus on Professional Tasks

Avoid being tempted to sneak personal tasks into the mix. Leave these for after hours or weekends. It's easy to become caught up in making a quick personal phone call or going onto social media to check your accounts. As tempting as this is, understand that the social media trap can rob you of an incredible amount of time that can be productive. Along with this comes surfing the internet for anything that's not project or work related. This saps hours of time that should be spent being productive.

Surfing the web and visiting YouTube or other non-essential sites is counter-productive. Remember that you're being paid to physically work and complete tasks on behalf of your employer, not to make use of their resources for your own personal gain.

Identify When You're Most Productive

Whether we realize it or not, we all have certain times of the day when we have more energy to get things done. Maybe you're an early riser and find that the silence allows you the opportunity to focus on completing tasks better, or you may prefer working late at night, once your children are asleep. Whatever system you choose, stick to it so that you manage to get the most out of the time you have available.

Avoid Trying to Multitask

Many of us believe that we can get much more accomplished if we multitask. This is simply not true. In fact, it takes more time for the brain to switch between multiple tasks than it does focusing all of your efforts and energy on completing one task at a time before moving on to the next. While this may require discipline and forcing yourself to focus a little harder on the task at hand, in the long run it will prove to be worthwhile in completing tasks on time. Developing a laser-like focus means doing whatever it takes to get the job done.

Getting tasks completed in a systematic way can help your brain process things more easily and makes the transition of moving from one task to another easier, because you're not still considering whether there's anything that's been left hanging or incomplete with previous tasks.

Your brain can only focus on a limited amount of things at the same time. This is why you should write things down on paper. It's getting the things out of your head and down on paper to make room for other thought processes to take place.

Take breaks

Reward yourself or take small breaks regularly to refocus and refresh your mind and body. Working from home is challenging enough, and you need to enforce similar guidelines and rules that you would have if you worked in a corporate office. There you would be entitled to regular tea or coffee breaks, as well as a set lunchtime. Schedule these same breaks into your day where you can get up, stretch your legs, maybe get some fresh air for a few minutes, grab something for lunch and then return to whatever you were doing.

Time Management = Self-discipline

Managing your time effectively is probably one of the areas where most people who work from home fail because they lack the self-discipline to work in exactly the same way as they would if they were working from an office. While there is certainly a bit more flexibility when it comes to working from home, it's not the time to slack off and avoid getting things done to meet targets and deadlines.

Being self-disciplined means getting up on time, showing up in your home office and being ready to put everything required into getting the job done every single day.

Chapter 8:

Become a Creature of

Habit

Why Routines?

In order to thrive and prosper working from your home-based office, you need to be able to get into a routine and stick to it. Make sure that you set your alarm as you would normally do if you were physically going to the office.

For me this was fairly easy as I had to do school runs before work, which made getting up early necessary. This forced me to have to get up and out everyday before official office hours would actually start.

'But I don't have kids—so what now?' I hear you ask. Setting a morning routine is still not only doable, but once you're in the habit, you'll begin to feel more positive about yourself and healthier in the long run.

Early Morning Routine

Go for a morning run in the fresh air or join a local gym. If you have a dog, this may be a great way to not only get exercise, but spend some quality time together in a suitable, dog-friendly environment. If you are out of shape right now, start small. Instead of a run, maybe start by taking a walk around your neighborhood for a half an hour and gradually build from there. Your walk could be extended further or turn into a slow jog as you begin to strengthen your muscles and build stamina. You'll find that the fresh air will do wonders for clearing cobwebs from some of your thinking, and you'll begin to feel more creative than ever before as a result of regular exercise and increased physical fitness.

Schedule Regular Early Morning Check-in Meetings

While this may not always be necessary, by implementing a daily early morning check-in meeting with your manager, supervisor or the team you're working with, you will know that you have to be there and bring you 'A-game' to the party. It will force you into the habit of being prepared for the day ahead and sticking to a regular schedule. When you've been doing this as long as I have, this isn't necessary, as both trust and routine are firmly established. However, at the early stages of working from home, this can definitely be a game-changer.

Other Early Morning Rituals

Adopting and implementing early morning rituals can help you build up solid routines. There are a number of ways to do this: from early morning meditation, to practicing yoga, to whatever works for you. Successfully implementing early morning rituals lies in discovering those that speak to you as an individual.

When implementing or adopting an early morning ritual, it needs to be something that resonates with you. Finding something on the Internet that's someone else's early morning game plan just won't work unless you have a 100% buy in that this ritual is exactly what you need; however, it may be useful to emulate another successful person's routine when trying to establish your own, picking and choosing what works for you and building on their list.

Other Routines and Boundaries

Before agreeing to work from your home office or remotely, you need to understand what's required in terms of routines, boundaries and expectations. It's better to get these down in writing before you make any hasty decisions or commit to something that you can't deliver further down the line.

Be Clear on Hours

Know what your working hours are going to be and stick to them. It's easy to become side-tracked, especially if you have your own office that is separated from the rest of the house. Time can often run away from you and you can become totally engrossed in what you're working on—all to the detriment of your family. Be aware of this and try and stick to regular hours as much as possible.

Take Regular Realistic Breaks

Take your lunch break at the same time as your colleagues would do in the office: that way you're working in a synchronized pattern and won't expect each other to be available for work during this time. Be realistic in the amount of time that you need 'off' to refresh and rejuvenate. If your job demands that you spend most of your time seated, make sure that your break is spent walking around, standing up or stretching, to ensure that your body remains in peak physical condition.

Get some fresh air. This may mean taking a walk in the garden, or shovelling some snow from your front entrance. Whatever you choose to do, your brain needs vital oxygen to function properly and you are responsible to ensure that this is something you get daily.

Sign Off and Out Daily

This is probably one of the most difficult routines to agree to and stick to because if you're addicted to your work, aka a workaholic, signing out is one of the hardest things you need to do each day. Imagine that you're working from the office. You know, where the clock watchers cannot wait for 10-minutes before official close of day. They are all packed up, computers signed out and switched off, and it's like a stampede to see who manages to get through the front door first.

While this may not be what you're aspiring to, it is necessary to be able to identify and understand when it's time to down tools for the day and close your office door until the morning. Sign off at the end of the day and then leave whatever work you haven't completed for the next day. As tempting as it is, quickly popping back into your office to send out an email after dinner is not an ideal scenario. Don't lose focus of why you're working from home in the first place.

Dress For Success

Photo Credit - Andrea Piacquadio from Pexels

Get dressed for work and show up ready for the day. It can be tempting to remain in your PJ's or sweats all day, or working while dressed extremely casually. From a psychological perspective this could actually have a negative impact on your work. You tend to produce results that are in line with the way that you feel about yourself. Let's face it, while it may make your life a whole lot easier working in your PJ's, it's not doing your self-esteem any good. They say that you're only as good as you feel, make sure that your dress and grooming portray this image, and the quality of your work will shine through.

Create Online Rapport

Create a regular online rapport with your colleagues by networking with them via online platforms like Skype or Zoom. This allows for and encourages healthy collaboration and can prevent any tension from forming because you're working remotely, and they're stuck in the office! When working on team-based projects, it's healthy to check in on a regular basis to ensure that everyone is on the same page. Regularly checking in, especially early in the day, dressed professionally, will help them see that you are taking your job seriously and that they can trust you even though you may not physically be in their direct line of sight every day.

Chapter 9:

Work / Life Balance

It's vital to be able to create a balance between your work and your home life. When you're working from a home-based office, it can be easy to become totally wrapped up in your work to the point where it's all-consuming. This is exactly what you're trying to avoid.

Separate Work and Home

If you go back to the beginning, to identify the actual reason why you wanted to work from home in the first place, you'll discover that nowhere does it actually mention that you wanted to work yourself into a coma!

You need to figure out how to separate your work life from your home life, and then manage to keep the two apart. My reasons for working from home were clear - I was tired of missing out on defining moments in the lives of my children. I wanted to be part of their lives, rather than sacrificing a lot of this valuable time commuting or wasting away in some 2 x 4 cubicle on the 6th floor, getting nowhere slowly!

When you quit for the day, make a point of leaving your work on your desk where it belongs. It's not going anywhere, and it will be waiting for you in the morning. Your family don't necessarily want to hear you droning on over dinner about some monotonous report that you've been working on. If you must talk about your work, keep the conversation lighthearted and to a bare minimum.

Getting the Balance Right

I'll be the first to admit that getting the work / life balance 100% correct takes time and effort. It takes discipline and learning when and where to set boundaries for yourself. Having work so close-by, it's often tempting to quickly go to work on a report that needs some finishing touches, or checking on emails before turning in for the night. Learning how to physically 'detach' and switch-off for the day has probably been one of the biggest challenges I've had to face.

This is a common thread that runs true for most people who work from home—the inability to switch off at the end of a busy day. This can negatively impact family and home life, and interfere with relationships with loved ones.

Getting the balance right means getting all the other basics that we've mentioned in previous chapters right:

- Creating a separate workspace that will serve ONLY as an office. Don't work from anywhere else in your home but from there, no matter how tempted you may be to take your laptop to your bedroom to quickly 'catch-up' on something. If you've signed off for the day, close your office door and only return once it's time for you to begin working again.
- Avoid logging into your work computer, iPhone or laptop the moment you wake up or during the night when you should be resting. Yes, working remotely has the benefit of providing you with 24/7 access, however, be realistic with the demands you're placing on yourself. If you were working from your corporate office, you'd probably head in, put your things down, greet people and make yourself a cup of coffee before even logging on for the day. Set similar boundaries for yourself in your home office. Give yourself time to plan your day and be realistic with your time.

While it's great for your family to have you home-based and around all the time, it can be pretty stressful for them if they see you seldom away from your dedicated workspace and never taking a break. Not to mention the added stress that you're placing on yourself to achieve targets that aren't necessarily realistic.

You can balance some of your personal time by scheduling activities or errands when you would normally take a break. While this may require some juggling, the pay-off in creating time to spend with family and loved ones is priceless. I'd give anything to have been able to experience each of my children's 'firsts', rather than being tied down to an office.

If you have the opportunity to work from home, set a schedule that provides sufficient time for family, along with work. Once you've managed to iron out a workable schedule that's both realistic and doable, stick with it.

Dedicate Family Time to Family

If you can devote yourself fully to your job during working hours, you should aim for the same kind of dedication when it comes to time spent with your family. They are the main reason why you chose to work from home in the first place! Decide what dedicated family time looks like. It may even be worthwhile consulting with your children over the dinner table, if they are old enough to communicate what their actual needs are.

While you might believe that being there to support them with school events or the early morning school run is enough, they may have some different ideas. When it comes to these conversations, listen to what they have to say while being fully focused, and see how you can accommodate them.

Often as parents we have the misconception that it's all about providing our children with materialistic things to make them feel better about themselves (or to prove to ourselves that we can). In reality, it's usually the simple things that they want, like trips down to the beach every Saturday, where you can spend quality time together as a family.

Find out what they want and need from you as a parent and then go out of your way to make those things happen.

Evening Rituals

When your children are still young, it's worth considering evening rituals that can help them realize the sacrifices that you're prepared to make for them, and that they're important to you. Spend quality time with them before bedtime, establishing evening rituals that they'll not only remember throughout their lives, but they may also carry them across to their own children someday.

Make a point of spending quality time with them. Read to them, or tell them stories of your own childhood. Children are malleable as clay during their formative years, and traditions that are established early on can have a huge impact on their lives. You need to let them know exactly how important they are to you.

This doesn't always need to be for hours on end, but some quality one-on-one time with each of your children before tucking them into bed can build a firm bond between you that will last a lifetime.

As they get too old to be tucked into bed with a story, you may want to continue with this quality one-on-one time, allowing them to confide in you about anything and everything. You will find that if your relationships are solid, your children will be more open with you whenever they have a problem or need advice. Always place your family first, no matter what!

Date Nights

While it's all fine and well to devote precious time each night to your children, don't forget about your spouse. They have probably stuck with you through thick and thin, and it's not always easy having to be around someone 24/7. To keep your marriage or relationship just as strong, set aside some time you can both enjoy alone together.

Whether you decide to commit to one evening every two weeks or one evening a month, carve out quality time the grown-ups can spend together. Make this time about each other and your relationship, not about discussing work or the children. It may be hard to do at first, but the more often you do this, the more you will find that your relationship continues to grow and develop. Think about things to do that aren't always obvious choices like going out for dinner: catch a movie or go to the theatre, or you may want to make an afternoon of it by attending a wine-tasting event or an art class.

Whatever it is, focus on each other and once again, try not to discuss work! A caveat here is to also avoid discussing the children. You and your partner may have differences of opinion, and the last thing you need to do is sabotage this time by fighting while you should be bonding.

Chapter 10:

Beat Procrastination - It

can be a Killer!

Procrastination is when you choose to do something else rather than doing what you really should be doing. It's delaying meeting targets and deadlines because you've found something that's more appealing or exciting to do with your time. Remember that we spoke earlier on about time being finite? This is a typical example of where when you choose to waste it on some frivolous activity, it can be harmful rather than helpful.

Accept Accountability

Working from home means that you and you alone are accountable for your day, your time and the level of productivity you achieve during this time. It's easy to fall into the various traps that the freedom of working from home automatically brings to the party.

If you're not organized or disciplined enough, you'll find endless excuses, like tackling household chores, rather than getting to the work that's actually required of you. Procrastination can rob you of time that you should be spending doing things that add to your productivity and getting the job done that needs to be done.

You need to accept that, from the moment you agreed to work from home, you accepted the accountability for your actions, and also the responsibility to get things done on behalf of the organization you represent, or your clients. If something goes wrong, you need to be adult enough to accept responsibility for your actions and avoid pointing fingers at others.

Avoid Activities that Waste Time

There are a number of obvious timewasters and activities that can be labelled as procrastination generators. One of them is definitely social media: it's easy to check your social media feed first thing in the morning, and before you know it, it's an hour later and you haven't even started working for the day. Social media is one of the major contributing factors to procrastination. Having said that, it's not the only thing that can stand in your way. Anything that can break your concentration and prevent you from focusing on completing a task can be labelled as procrastination.

Here are several other forms of procrastination that I've noticed over the years:

- **Television:** don't set up your workstation anywhere near a television. You're bound to get distracted or tempted to switch to watching one of your favorite programs (just for a few minutes!). If you need to catch up on global markets and the news, carve space out at the beginning of your day, while you're enjoying your morning coffee, to watch the news, then switch off the TV and get to business!
- **Radio:** if you enjoy background noise or listening to music as a means of being productive, create a mix of some of your favorite music, and have it playing in the background, as long as it's going to help you remain focused on the task at hand, rather than distracting from your work. Many people need white noise in the background in order to function efficiently. Avoiding procrastination should be about creating an environment that's as productive as possible.
- **YouTube and other websites:** unless this is part of your job, avoid these like the plague.

YouTube is sneaky, they run from one video directly onto the next and while your original intention was to only watch one thing, before you blink, you've been online for several hours! Don't get sucked into any website that can be potentially time consuming and distracting.

- **Household chores:** if you happen to work in an open plan environment that's attached to your lounge, dining room or kitchen, anything that needs to be done around the home can become a distraction and present itself as the perfect reason to procrastinate getting things done! Whether it's simply putting a load of dirty laundry into the washing machine or stacking dishes in the dishwasher, each of these activities take time and remove you from your work.

- **External noise:** try and minimize the overall effects that external noise has on your ability to concentrate on your work. This may require some flexibility when raising a young family (which is quite possibly your reason for working from home in the first place). Work around it as much as possible, or make sure that your office is closed off and disruptions are minimized.

Maintain Focus

Whenever you feel as though you're beginning to lose focus on what needs to be done work-wise, consider how you would react if you were in that 2 x 4 cubicle at the office? You wouldn't even dream about doing any of these things, because you'd be fully focused on doing what's required of you, considering that you're at work and being paid to perform or function as such.

Work from home as though you were in the office. Imagine that you have a manager watching over your shoulder and double-checking your every move. If you want to continue to be trusted and earn the respect of those you work for and with, this is exactly what it's going to take. Imagine that they can physically monitor every single keystroke that you're making on your computer, every email, every telephone conversation, every report … I think you get the idea!

Be Trustworthy

If you find that you're the type of individual that needs to take regular breaks throughout the day to break the monotony of work, set a timer for yourself. Take a 15-minute break and put that load of washing in the machine ... at the end of the 15-minutes, return to your office and continue where you left off.

Be the type of individual that your client or corporation can trust implicitly. If you need to take several breaks, your work hours may stretch out beyond the regular 9 to 5 grind. It may mean that you need to begin working at 7 in the morning to make up for all the short breaks you take. Be honest in the amount of work that you're putting in. This will not only make you a valued employee, but it will result in management, clients and colleagues being able to trust your commitment and dedication to all that you do.

Chapter 11:

Reward Yourself - Go for

the Carrot

Nobody enjoys working for the sake of working. Let's face it, there's always a reward of some description that's attached to everything we do. For most, when working for large corporations, you're working for a salary at the end of each month, or that additional productivity bonus that's been promised if you meet your targets for the financial quarter. Why not set up a similar reward system for yourself that will help keep you motivated and increase your level of productivity?

This could be anything from meeting a specific deadline to closing a deal successfully! Sometimes these mini milestones are what can set you apart from your colleagues and provide you with that slight advantage.

The Carrot vs. the Stick

I'm not advocating that these rewards be anything grandiose like brand new cars or trips overseas, but small, realistic 'treats' that you wouldn't normally consider instead. It's figuring out how to motivate yourself with a carrot rather than a stick, and we all know that this form of motivation is much healthier than operating out of fear and stress.

Some of these rewards could include:

- Catching up with a friend at a local coffee shop during one of your breaks.
- Enjoying an Indian head massage at a local spa.
- Rewarding yourself with a new hairstyle.
- Spoiling yourself with a new item of clothing that you normally wouldn't buy.
- Adding that special bottle of perfume or cologne to your shopping basket the next time you're out.
- If you love reading, stopping in at your local bookstore and purchasing that latest bestseller you've had your eye on for sometime.
- Treating yourself to a hot stone massage as a way to destress.

- Booking a manicure or pedicure at your favorite salon.
- Catching up on your favorite series on Netflix.
- Going for an invigorating walk in your neighborhood or along the beach.

The potential rewards are literally endless. Be creative and think of those things that you'd really like to do, but seldom find the time to do. Maybe it's actually taking some time out to experience new things or learning a new hobby.

Involve the Family

Photo Credit - Delcho Dichev from Pexels

To become really motivated to achieve a deadline, reach a target or close a deal, you may want to involve all members of your family with a slightly bigger carrot. These rewards also don't necessarily need to be extravagant or over the top. Don't promise anything that you know you could never deliver. Sometimes spending quality time together as a family is rewarding enough.

By involving family members, you'd be amazed at how quickly they'll get on board with your work project and begin following up with you or nagging you to get it done. These rewards can be things like a dinner out, or taking the entire family to watch a new release at the cinema … whatever it is, think about what you'd really enjoy and then stick with it. Chase after the carrot with all that you have, but remember that for the donkey to remain fully motivated, he needs to enjoy the carrot every once in a while.

Request Team Incentives

If you are working for a large corporation and you happen to be part of a project team, request a team based incentive from management. This may be slightly harder to pull off because you're looking for some type of recognition or reward for a number of people; however, if the project you're working on is of any value to the company, this might just be the answer to

getting all of your teammates on board and collaborating towards a common, positive goal, rather than working against one another. It's a way to motivate everyone to meet targets and objectives set and produce results before the time, rather than having to beg anyone who may be dragging their heels.

Once again, this doesn't need to be money (although a bonus is an excellent motivator): it can be time off in lieu of a target reached, or a meal out, things that a company can easily expense and recover without it impacting their bottom-line.

Chapter 12:

Communication - I'm here and I'm working hard, honest!

Working independently, unsupervised from a remote location requires high levels of trust and integrity. One of the ways to prove that you're doing what you're being tasked to do is through regular, thorough communication. Whether this communication is with the teams that you work with or with your immediate superiors, it tells them that you're available, you're doing whatever it is that you've been tasked to do and that you're a resource that they can rely on.

Integrity is greatly admired in today's workforce. It not only displays a high level of trustworthiness, but it confirms that you're putting your money where your mouth is!

Check in Regularly

Photo Credit - Fauxels from Pexels

Checking in with management and teams that you may be collaborating with on a regular basis is an excellent way to make sure that work is synchronized, and that everyone is on task. Advancements in technology have made it really easy to keep in touch with team members, even when you're working remotely.

Applications like Slack allow you to communicate in real time with others on your team, and it's easy to see whether you're checking in on your message boards or not. It also provides you with a way to communicate

with any single individual to advise them of updates, request information or simply acknowledge that you're on top of things from your end. I personally use Microsoft Teams, which for myself is one of the best possible tools to be using, when you're in my situation, working from the UK for an operation that's USA based.

Be Honest at all Times

Be honest and open in your communications at all times: if you're battling with something or don't believe that you'll be able to meet a particular deadline, communicate this through to the relevant individuals working with you. It's easier to make contingency plans beforehand, rather than trying to close the barn door once the horse has already bolted!

Share tasks that you're working on with your team, so that everyone's on the same page and knows who's responsible for what. Don't assume that someone else is completing a task that you know needs to be handled but doesn't appear on the list of things to do. Don't be afraid to speak up and question roles and responsibilities in order to gain total clarity and transparency.

Commit to Regular Facetime

Schedule regular one-on-one face time with management. This may require commuting to the office once or twice a month in order to provide regular updates and physical reporting. This can strengthen relationships with other teammates as they see you physically in the workplace from time to time, and it also gives you time to break out of the isolation and monotony that can cause you to fall into a bit of a funk when working completely on your own.

When you're due to have these meetings, make sure that you're prepared with all your facts and information well beforehand so that valuable time isn't wasted scrambling to find documentation of files when you ought to be meeting.

Draw up an agenda for these meetings and then stick to it. Don't go off-book and start discussing things that are irrelevant, respect the time that management is setting aside to meet with you. If you need to discuss other things, reschedule another appointment when it's convenient for them.

Use Technology

Make use of applications and tools available to communicate with other employees to keep them posted. Some of these applications that have been specifically designed to assist teams working in collaboration with one another are Slack, as discussed above, and Skype messenger. Being able to communicate with one another in real time, or setting preferences for when you're not available is easy to do and make managing teams in remote locations an absolute breeze.

Zoom has replaced a lot of video conferencing that would have been handled before by Skype; whatever your preference, or the preference of the company that you're working for, you can make use of this technology when communicating with others.

Photo Credit - Christina Morillo from Pexels

Chapter 13:

Meetings from Home -

Acceptable Etiquette

Video conferencing makes being able to communicate effectively with one another over vast distances, even across continents. Making use of productivity tools that are currently available decrease these distances and allow for real-time face-to-face communication. While you may be in different time zones, finding common ground and times that suit everyone is relatively easy to do.

When it comes to these meetings, there are a few guidelines and correct etiquette that should be followed to ensure that you come across professionally at all times.

Some things to take into consideration are the following:

Equipment:

- Does your equipment support the functionality required?
- Does your hardware support a decent webcam and sound that's clear enough for communicating effectively?
- You may prefer to invest in a headset with a built-in microphone to reduce background noise and assist with clear communication from your side.

Environment:

- Choose to use an environment that is well lit and has very little shadows.
- Consider what's behind you during your call and keep it professional. The ideal scenario is to have a plain background that's not cluttered in any way. Items in the background can be a major distraction, especially when communicating long distance. Simplify your background and keep spaces tidy, a healthy plant or tasteful painting is ideal. I happened to

be watching a video on YouTube a while ago where the individual presenting the information wanted to come across as being a 'high-powered, successful, trend-setting individual' and while all of these things may be true, the video was shot with a glass window from a high-rise as a background where the lights from all the passing traffic made it virtually impossible to focus on the message he was trying to get across. In this instance, he would have been more convincing sitting behind a desk with a blank wall behind him. This single incident has made me re-evaluate the way that my own home office is set up for video-conferencing calls.

- Make sure that members of your family are forewarned that you're going to be on a conference call and that you're not to be disturbed. There's nothing as unprofessional as having to excuse yourself because the family dog keeps wanting to jump on your lap throughout your meeting! This may require putting a 'Do Not Disturb' sign on your door, and explaining to younger children that if and when that sign is on the door, they find something else to do, rather than demanding your attention at that time.

Photo Credit - Curtis Adams from Pexels

Dress appropriately

Even though you're working from home, dress professionally for video conferencing meetings. You will know whether your meeting requires formal work attire or whether you can go smart casual instead—whatever you do, avoid having a meeting in your sweats and a T-shirt, unless you're part of a rock band checking in with your record label!

Rules to follow when it comes to dress code are as follows:

- Do your homework and find out what the dress code is for the company that you're video conferencing with. These are often unwritten rules and may require a bit of digging. Think about big brands like Apple, Microsoft, Amazon, or Google: they all have a certain style of dressing. The correct rule when it comes to video conferencing is to dress one step up from their standard dress code.
- If you are meeting with senior business executives, go the suit and tie route to be safe. There's nothing that says 'I mean business' more than the way that you attend to your personal grooming.
- Avoid over the top hairstyles and accessories, they are totally unnecessary and can sometimes send the completely wrong message. Keep it simple, yet professional.

Always Be Prepared

Be prepared at all times, you never know when you may need to accept an urgent, unscheduled video conference call from either management or a client who's in desperate need of your attention or advice. Even if it means that the top half of your dress code is professional, or can become professionally looking within a few short minutes, consider this route. It may mean leaving a freshly ironed shirt and tie in your office that you can quickly slip on before a conference call, or a tailored jacket that can make you look as though you are professionally dressed and can be taken seriously.

It's something small that can however make a huge difference in how you are perceived by others out there, especially when you're representing a large corporation or international concern.

Chapter 14:

Security

Ensuring that proprietary information is kept safe at all times is one of the key factors to consider when working remotely. It's easier monitoring networks and protecting information within larger corporations, as data is on site and can be backed up on secure servers on a daily basis if needs be. Keeping confidential information safe at all times is a habit that one has to get into when working remotely.

Passwords on Hardware

Security starts with your actual hardware and accessibility. Make sure that your computer is password protected and locked at all times. This may sound like I'm stating the obvious, but don't write your passwords down anywhere that they can easily be found and don't choose passwords that are easy to figure out. Avoid choosing passwords like your date of birth or a nickname for someone close to you: these are easy to hack and the last thing you need is for proprietary information to be compromised.

Try and set up multi-layered encryption, making it more difficult for people to hack into your system, especially when your computer is at home. The reason for large corporations being more difficult to hack into is because they have firewalls everywhere, and normally operate on networks with large mainframes. While this is all fine and well for them in their corporate office, you need to be realistic that working offsite doesn't provide you with the same level of protection.

Lock Away Documents

Any printed documents that should be kept confidential should be filed under lock and key, and if work needs to be destroyed, it simply cannot be crumpled up and thrown in the trash. Invest in a shredder and use it whenever necessary.

If you cannot place confidential documents into a filing cabinet that has a lock and key, the next best thing is to physically lock your office door whenever you leave it and unlock it when you return. This is not to say that someone in your family is likely to be guilty of corporate espionage, but it's protecting anything that you're working on from being compromised in any way whatsoever.

Choose the Right Antivirus Software

Carefully consider the antivirus software protection for your system. While there are a lot of open source products available for free, with something as important as antivirus protection, it's way better to choose a paid plan. Many of these are also available on monthly options, making it affordable for small businesses. Many people opt for the free, open source software available on the net to keep their data secure, however, should something go wrong, this could be an extremely costly exercise. Paid, quality antivirus software comes with regular patches and security upgrades on a regular basis. These upgrades are free and can be scheduled for times when you're not actually working on your system, therefore not interfering with your workflow at all.

VPNs (Virtual Private Networks)

Ensure that you have VPNs for connectivity security. This is extremely important when working remotely from home as this presents a higher likelihood of being targeted by hackers. For most large corporations this will automatically be set up for you, and you may need to provide the company's IT department with remote access for upgrades every so often; this will ensure that your data is safe though.

For sole proprietors or entrepreneurs though, going with monthly subscription options for VPNs such as CyberGhost, Nord VPN and Surf Shark could present cost-effective solutions to ensuring that your computer is protected. If you are self-employed, these costs can also be added into your expenses when submitting your annual tax returns.

Avoid Open Wi-Fi Networks

When it comes to working remotely, beware of logging in on public Wi-Fi networks, as these aren't always protected: by using them without thinking, you can open your entire system up for viruses, malware and hacking. This is possibly one of the biggest challenges that remote workers face. It's as easy as meeting up with a client at a local coffee shop that offers a free Wi-Fi service, and before you know it, your system's been hacked.

If you must meet up with clients and you need to log onto the internet for any reason whatsoever, it's best to have your own portable router that's secure, so that you are protected from any malicious attacks or security breaches that could possibly occur. You will probably find that the company you're working for will be only too happy to provide you with a mobile router or an internet dongle if you need to meet with clients off site on a regular basis, rather than costing them millions in losing important information.

Encrypt Files and Back up Regularly

Try and encrypt your files as far as you can, and back up your information on a regular basis, storing this back-up device safely, whether it's on an external hard drive, or cloud based. The more you're able to protect your data, the more difficult it becomes for competing companies to get their hands on any of your data. It also secures your information in the event of unforeseen circumstances, such as burglary. When it comes to protecting information for your employer, treat it as if it were your very own and as if you actually have a physical share in their business. When you view a business operation this way, you get a much broader overview of what's really important and the true value of data and information.

The actual cost of replacing data can run into tens of thousands of dollars, not to mention actual man-hours spent having to try and recapture or replace lost information.

Chapter 15:

Beating Loneliness

Loneliness can be one of the most debilitating aspects of working from home. Think about it, most of your day is spent in an office or in your dedicated workspace on your own, working hard to get the job done. As individuals, we need human interaction with others in order to keep our mental health in check and to avoid a psychological slump, moving into a state of depression.

Remaining emotionally healthy is also in the best interests of all the people in your life, both those you work with and interact with daily, as well as members of your family. It's necessary for you to be able to function and bring your 'A-game' to the table every single day. So, how can you deal with these feelings of loneliness? How can you recognize them, and do something before they become a genuine threat to your productivity and stand in the way of you being effective?

Here are several tips and techniques to avoid loneliness:

Get Out Daily

Make sure that you take some time every single day to get out into the world, where you have a chance to interact with other people. This could be as simple as going to a local coffee shop or internet café and working from there for an hour or so. Simply having others around you will immediately lift your mood and help you realize that there are others out there and you're not really on your own.

Join a Gym

We've briefly discussed this as part of a morning routine; however it is a way of not only keeping the body healthy, but the mind as well. The social interaction of working out with others around you can restore a sense of being connected with the rest of the world once more. After all, feelings of loneliness are usually caused by lack of human interaction. Something as simple as being able to greet others around you, or sharing a smile can boost your endorphins and make you feel better about your current situation.

Photo Credit - wokandpix from Pixabay

Listen to the Radio or Podcasts

The mere fact that you are making use of your auditory senses will also help create the sensation that you're not alone. Often having the radio or music playing in the background can help your work along and motivate you to get into a creative rhythm. Podcasts or suitable audio books can also provide you with the necessary motivation required to get down to work. I listen to regular radio shows, which also form part of my daily routine.

Set up an IM System

When working remotely for a larger organization, instant messaging systems can be a means of communicating with others, therefore feeling less lonely and vulnerable to feeling as though there's nobody out there who cares about you. Being able to recognize when you are feeling lonely is important as this could potentially prevent you from spiraling downwards, where loneliness can turn to anxiety or depression.

Spend Time in Nature

If you're really beginning to feel the walls closing in, take some time out and go for a walk. Take a break and spend time gaining a better appreciation for the nature that is all around you. If you happen to have a dog, this may be a great opportunity to take your dog for a walk or a run. There's nothing quite like a 45-minute break spent in the outdoors to get you motivated once again and help you reconnect with yourself.

Team Building / Training

Photo Credit - Mohamed Hassan from Pixabay

Attend regular team building or training sessions that your employer offers, so that you have the opportunity to reconnect with other employees of the company as well as teammates. It's healthy to ensure that communication channels and relationships with those that you work with remain strong despite the fact that you're working remotely. By showing that you're willing to remain connected, you display a genuine interest and concern for the wellbeing of your teammates, as well as other members of the organization.

Use Video Conferencing

As discussed above, Zoom or Skype are ideal ways to be able to connect with colleagues and customers regularly. There are a number of other tools at your disposal that you can use to help you reach out and communicate effectively. Instead of texting, pick up the phone and actually have a conversation. You'd be amazed by how much better you will feel. Remember that no man is an island, we all need to feel that we matter and that we are connected with others.

Interconnectivity can also serve as a means to gain clarity from those we're working with or for. It can open channels of communication that are vital for the success in any business; we need to make use of as many of the tools that are available to us as we can to help us overcome any feelings of loneliness that we may experience from time to time.

Chapter 16:

Home Health

It's important to take care of your physical health when you're working from a home office. Because you're in a situation where you're working where you live, where you eat, where you sleep and where you socialize with others, it can become very easy to lose focus of those things that really matter. Your health is one of these.

Working Close to the Kitchen

During the first 6 months of working from home, I put on a significant amount of weight. I was constantly eating all the wrong things and did it as a form of reward. Having easy access to snacks and treats is something you need to try and avoid at all costs, as excessive eating can definitely be a negative aspect of working from home.

It becomes way too easy to get up to stretch your legs and walk by the kitchen for a quick snack on the way back to your office. If this is the case, remove any and all unhealthy snacks from where you can reach them. Better still, get your spouse to hide them from you, so you're not tempted to eat and end up packing on the pounds just like I did.

Manage your schedule and stick to your tea or coffee breaks as you normally would do if you were working from an actual office. Stay as far away from junk food, sweets and treats as possible. Your body will thank you for it later. Gaining weight is one thing, but trying to lose it and keeping it off afterwards can prove to be challenging.

We've established that your body definitely needs to be able to rest and recharge throughout the day in order to be productive. Find something else to do for each of these breaks, making healthier choices in the long-run.

Replace the Urge to Eat

There are a number of things that you can do to ensure you don't overeat while working from home. Some of these include:

- Instead of heading for the cookie jar, take your dog for a quick walk around the block and back again.

- Reward yourself with things other than food. If you've managed to meet a deadline or close a deal, reward yourself with something that you really want, rather than junk food or anything else that's detrimental to your health. You might want to set a goal to complete several tasks over a number of days and reward yourself with some much-needed rest and relaxation with your family at the beach for an afternoon. Other incentives could include spending time with friends that you seldom get to meet up with.

- Avoid eating as a means of rewarding yourself. One way to do this is by replacing all the junk food, snacks and cookies in your home with fresh fruit and vegetables, yoghurt and other foods that you can snack on that are going to improve your health rather than adding to your waistline!

- We've already covered the importance of getting regular exercise and possibly signing up with a local gym as a means of interacting with others while improving your physical fitness and mental health at the same time. Realistically however, if you're only looking at taking a short break, to rejuvenate and realign your thinking, physically getting in your car and going to a gym for a workout is not really an option for you. Consider setting up a mini home gym where you can take a short break if necessary, you'd be amazed how a mini workout can make you feel more positive and ready to take on the world once more.

- Be kind to yourself and take regular short breaks away from sitting in front of the screen. It's easy to become so totally engrossed in whatever task needs doing to remain glued to your seat and computer for extended lengths of time without resting. This can lead to health hazards such as back problems (especially if your seat is not ergonomically correct), eye strain, water retention and other circulatory problems if you're not getting up and taking regular breaks. It's easy to get caught up 'in the zone' of your work, especially if you're running with an exciting project that you're passionate about, or you have an idea that you're scared will disappear if you take a 5-minute break!

Recognize When You Need a Break

The truth is that none of us are robots and we are all susceptible to things like 'burn out' if we don't take proper care of ourselves when we're working from home. If you've drawn up your work schedule, or your list of priorities for the day and you're working according to a set number of hours, take the breaks necessary at the agreed upon times, take your lunch time as though you were in the office and learn to 'switch off' and log out from work once the work day is done.

It's easy to become sucked into working longer than normal hours when you're operating in a different time zone than your head office and you need to be available for webinars or video conference calls after hours; this time should then be deducted from your normal working pattern.

How Working From Home Can Be More Efficient

In a study conducted by Stanford University, Professor Nick Bloom discovered that individuals working from home were not only more productive, but they got more done, took fewer sick days than their counterparts in the workplace and worked longer hours than regular employees (Stanford Business, Insights, Researchers, 2012).

Try and find a happy medium between getting your work done, spending the right amount of time behind your desk, taking regular and frequent breaks and avoiding foods that aren't good for you.

Chapter 17:

Self-Respect

It's important to take care of your physical appearance and personal hygiene even though you're working from home. I know that it's tempting to be able to walk around the house in your sweats and slippers all day long while you're working, but consider what message you're sending about yourself to those you associate with or come into contact with throughout the day.

Show Up Dressed Professionally Daily

Make a habit of always getting dressed for work, no matter what—you never know when an emergency conference call may be scheduled, and the last thing you need is having to frantically hustle to look the part. Ultimately, you want to do everything in your power not to create the wrong impression of your current situation. Despite what the other person is wearing, make sure that you're always presentable. Remember that in many instances you're the face of the company that you represent, so make the first impression a lasting and positive one.

I know of many individuals who just put a shirt and tie on and are comfortable wearing their sweatpants during a conference call. The problem with this is that you may be asked to go and fetch something ... talk about an embarrassing situation!

Suit and Tie?

I once learned that someone I know thought I was doing nothing, sitting at home, not working, on benefits. This gave me a huge wake-up call, and I've made it a point ever since to always present myself professionally, and to be ready for every situation at a moment's notice. A guy I used to know would get up every day, put on his full suit and go work from his shed (which was his office) for the day. He would only go back to the house at lunch time, and would only get out of his work clothes once he had physically clocked off at the end of the working day.

He had created clear boundaries for himself and could see the difference between being at home and actually being productive and professional. Even though his work environment was a shed in his backyard, he was disciplined enough to get dressed professionally in a suit and tie every day.

First Impressions

Remember that first impressions are lasting impressions. There's a saying that says that to be successful you need to get up, get dressed and show up! This pretty much sums up how important it is to look the part, even though you're working from a home office.

There's a psychological reason behind placing value in the way that you dress and carry yourself each day. When you are dressed professionally, you have the tendency to behave more professionally. Mooching off in your sweats all day long creates the feeling that you're actually on holiday and getting into 'work mode' can be more challenging.

Your physical appearance should also be taken into consideration. Ensure that you're neatly groomed and ready for anything to happen. Get into the habit of bathing or showering before getting ready to face the day. Your physical appearance has a direct impact on your work. When you feel good about yourself, naturally the quality of your work will reflect this. Conversely, when you don't care about your personal appearance or how you look while working, your work is likely to be just as mediocre.

If you want to be taken seriously by your employer, or even as a solopreneur, or entrepreneur working for yourself, it's worth spending a bit of time on your physical appearance. When you dress the part, you act the part!

Find the Balance

Consider the audience that you're working with and remember to keep it professional at all times. If you want them to take you seriously, dress the part.

Avoid any hairstyles that could come across as being unprofessional. Same goes for things like body piercings, that may define who you are on a social level, but have no place in a high-powered boardroom discussion, unless you're working for an art gallery or creative team where this type of culture is embraced and accepted. Getting it exactly right the first time may not be easy if you're brand new to working remotely, without being associated with the company or client before then. Those 'unwritten' rules I mentioned when it comes to dress code come into play here. When in doubt, ask before you end up embarrassed by not being fully prepared.

Chapter 18:

Staying in the Game

through Training

Most companies offer training days on a regular basis to upskill their staff. As a remote worker, grab each of these opportunities with both hands as and when they're presented to you. Even though you may feel that you already have the knowledge pertaining to a specific skill set, there's always an opportunity for you to gain additional knowledge.

Inhouse Training Courses

Many of these training sessions are based at the company's head office or at a regional office that's closest to you. Take advantage of training days as a means of getting out of your home office and being able to connect with colleagues and other members of your team. Even if you walk away having gained only one single simple concept, the training will have been worth it. Attending also proves to colleagues and management that you are willing to further yourself and do whatever it takes to be part of their team.

Upskill Yourself

Adopting a 'know it all' attitude isn't healthy for anyone in any organization, this is why it's vital to show management within your business that you take your work seriously and that you are grateful for opportunities to learn new things or gain new experience. If there's a training program that you believe would add value to your position within the organization, don't be afraid to speak up and request to be upskilled. Managers respect those who are ambitious and can recognize when they need help to improve.

Search for Online Training Opportunities

Gaining new skills in a rapidly changing business landscape is an important opportunity that you want to be seen utilizing to your full advantage. If your company happens to offer online learning opportunities, take them. There are diverse online learning platforms that can allow you to further expand your knowledge in a specific area of learning. An excellent example of a cost-effective online institution that offers thorough and diverse training courses is Udemy.

While your employer may not be willing to send you on any old random course that you request to go on, if you can present a valid argument as to how the business could potentially benefit from this training further down the line, you might just have a shot at getting what you want.

Industry Forums and Events

Industry forums often have annual or biannual meetings where they have guest speakers prepared to share their knowledge and insights on different ways of doing business. Attending some of these meetings will provide you with the opportunity of networking with like-minded professionals in your industry. This often leads to sharing of ideas and being able to come up with innovative solutions relevant to your business.

Make the most of these events. They could provide you with opportunities to network with and meet influential individuals who might be game changers within your industry. By turning your nose up at these invitations or events, you may never know what potential opportunities you're throwing away. Events are the perfect occasion to make a name for yourself, your team, as well as your organization you represent.

Audio Books

Audio books are an excellent source of training: they are available on Audible, for example, at reasonable prices. In addition, free training can often be found on YouTube. If you prefer physically reading rather than using the audio option, applications such as AnyBooks and PDFDrive offer downloads of thousands of books of all sorts of genres absolutely free.

Develop an Attitude of Lifelong Learning

The fact is that learning, adapting, and gaining new skills is something that should be happening on a daily basis because the world of technology is morphing daily. If you aren't physically doing something about improving your skill set or gaining additional knowledge that's going to set you apart from the competition or the rest of the world, you're going to be left behind, and playing catch up can be extremely hard to do.

Adopt an attitude of lifelong learning, where you strive to improve yourself in some small way constantly. Set your sights on learning at least one new thing every single day, that way, by the end of each year you will be able to say that you've added 365 new things to your skillset. Once you've developed the habit of gaining additional knowledge every day, you'll virtually be set for life. You never know when one of these gems of information will come in handy and help boost you up the corporate ladder.

Chapter 19:

Cabin Fever

Overcoming the feeling that you're stuck on a hamster wheel with your work cycle going a little something like this: 'I live here, I eat here, I work here, I sleep here–REPEAT,' can be extremely challenging. Your life could easily be represented by a programmed cycle on your washing machine. It's easy to feel as though the walls are closing in and you have nowhere to hide!

There are a number of solutions to reduce and eliminate the sensations that you're experiencing. Some ideas to get you started are:

Call it quits over weekends

Whatever happens, avoid working over weekends at all costs! Think about it for a moment: unless your company was physically burning to the ground, how often would you actually be required to come into the office after hours or on weekends?

Change of scenery

Get out and about on the weekends. Spend time with your family and loved ones doing things that are new and exciting. Taking a drive to a nearby museum or aquarium might be just what the family needs. For most of us, we live in places that are steeped in history and tradition. Spend some time scouring the internet for some of these interesting places within driving distance and make a day of it. You never know what precious memories will be created by doing so, as well as being able to forge stronger social bonds with members of your family.

Look out for local events

If you have location services enabled on your phone, Facebook will automatically send you information on events taking place in and around your vicinity (sometimes these can be up to 3 months in advance). Decide as a family whether any of these events are suitable and that can be done together: they can range from music concerts to dog expos, from book releases and wine tastings, to cycle tours and moonlight yoga, so there's something for everyone! We once spent a memorable afternoon, which came about completely by accident. We ended up taking part in a stonemason event and now we have our family names etched inside a block in one of the walls of Canterbury Cathedral.

The whole point is to find something to do that's going to take you out of your home, as well as possibly your comfort zone, and is going to present you with the opportunity to grow together as a family.

Take a class

Maybe you've never tried your hand at scuba diving. Find a local instructor near you and book a class for yourself and your family. Do something that's going to challenge you but excite you at the same time. You never know when something like this could come in handy. Maybe you would like to explore something new, like an art class, which may also serve to relax you.

Enjoy the outdoors

Even if you're homebound for the weekend, spend as much time as possible outdoors in the fresh air. Invite friends over for a barbeque and socialize. It will do you so much good, being able to connect with others and interact socially once again . We often go for long country walks in woodland areas near where we live together, which we all enjoy together as a family.

LAY OFF THE WORK!

Whatever you choose to do over the 48-hour period between Friday afternoon and Monday morning, avoid work at all costs. It's easy to slip into the habit of working one Friday evening, which then turns into working all Friday evenings and adding finishing touches on a Saturday morning. This in turn can become a whole day affair on a Saturday, and before you know it, you're working through entire weekends at the expense of your family relationships. Chances are that you can't bill for the extra hours, and therefore the only winner in this scenario is your employer. You start the new week off without having had any time to recharge your batteries and you're well and truly on the road to 'burnout,' both emotionally and physically.

Weekends off are earned

This should really be common sense for anyone who works, weekends off are actually mandatory and this time has been earned as a result of the hours that you've put in during the preceding week. Don't short-change yourself, or think that someone is going to notice that you've been putting in all the extra hours. As long as your work is on task and up to date, find something fun to do with your family and take a break!

Chapter 20:

Breaktime / Recess

When it comes to breaktimes and recess, this all boils down to effective time management and how you've established the ground rules right from the outset. Your time should be clearly scheduled, with both a clear start and finish time that's been clearly communicated through to management, or to your clients and customers.

Schedule Breaks Throughout the Day

The body and mind are also only able to focus and concentrate for a certain amount of time without taking a break. Schedule these breaks as they are needed throughout the day. Even if you are sitting in a comfortable, ergonomically correct office chair, it's still important to get up and stretch your legs every so often. Being able to physically stretch your arms, neck and back muscles are also important.

Go for a short break by taking a brisk walk to prevent any stiffness from building up – this is also a great way to avoid the cookie jar that I told you about earlier on.

One of the main reasons for scheduling regular breaks during the day so that you can be more effective at what you are doing.

Avoiding Eye Strain

Staring at the computer screen all day places strain on your eyes: give them a break every once in a while, by physically standing up and walking away from the computer.

Make Time to Exercise

Make time to exercise your entire body either first thing in the morning or after work at night. We are each different and have natural peaks and lows. Peaks are represented by when we are able to get the most done: for some of us this is first thing in the morning, while for others, it's later in the day or even into the wee hours of the night. There's nothing wrong with working at hours and times when you're likely to be most effective; as a matter of fact, it's in your best interest to do so.

Work to a Schedule

Whatever schedule works for you, set it down in writing and if you're reporting to an organization, make sure that they're aware of those times when you're able to do your best work. Make sure that you still meet your weekly quota of hours that are necessary and stipulated in your contract, so that nobody can accuse you of slacking off or not performing.

Stick with the scheduled breaks as best you can, even if you need to set two alarms on your phone, one for the beginning of your break and the other for the end of your break. Repeat this same process for your lunch time routine as well as other regular breaks during the day.

By stretching regularly and sticking with your regular breaks throughout the day, you'll find that you're able to concentrate a whole lot easier and work will flow better. You're less likely to suffer from things like eye strain or back problems, muscle soreness or fatigue because you've given your body a series of mini rests and respites during the day.

Chapter 21: Housework

Not having to waste time commuting in and out of the office each day definitely leaves you with extra time on your hands. While this is a huge advantage, you can become easily distracted by housework that needs to be done. This could lead to a form of procrastination and putting off what needs to be done by choosing to do housework instead.

Housework = Procrastination

Accept that there will always be something around the home that needs doing, whether this is hanging out washing, ensuring that your kitchen remains clean and tidy, or replacing the linen on your bed. Working from home can make it too easy for boundaries to become blurred between getting down to business during business hours and taking time out to do other things that need to be done but will inevitably distract you.

Even choosing to do household chores when you should be taking breaks during your workday is not ideal. A break is meant to provide you with time to rest and prepare for the next wave of work that needs to be done. Shifting this focus onto doing housework instead doesn't let you rest and recharge effectively, and you could easily spend way more time on your chore than your break should be, becoming engrossed in doing things that can be done after hours.

Separate Business from Housework

While getting things done around the house may feel rewarding at the time, it certainly doesn't move you any closer towards achieving your work goals or completing those things on your list of items to action throughout the day. Learn to separate what needs to be done in and around the home from what needs to be done for work: the two should never compete for your time. As soon as you find yourself being tempted to clean the kitchen 'quickly' while you're supposed to be having a 15-minute scheduled break, you may need to re-evaluate and redefine your working hours to examine how fully committed you are to working from home.

Be Highly Disciplined

Working from home requires discipline, and once you begin factoring other things into the mix, any routines or plans that you had originally scheduled for working from home tend to go a bit awry. Hold out to your original routine, clarifying that there is a complete distinction between your actual working hours and doing housework. For many marriages where one partner works from home and the other commutes to an office, there can be a lack of communication or understanding regarding the demands on the time of the party who is working from home. This needs to be communicated effectively so that the roles don't become completely skewed. Your partner needs to understand that your work requires just as big a commitment from you as if you were reporting to an office. This is every bit applicable even if you are working for yourself from a home office.

Reasons for working from home need to also be clearly defined. If one of your main motivations to be there is so that you can be part of the school run in the morning and afternoon, and be more supportive to your kids whenever they have a hockey game or swim meet after school, that's great, but somewhere, this time needs to be reallocated and worked back in.

Mutual Understanding

The truth is that nobody ever achieved success by coasting through life: it's going to take diligence, effort and mutual understanding by all parties. Those partnerships that are able to stand the test of time in a working from home scenario are those that share household chores together outside of agreed upon work time. Remember that you are in control of your day. If you feel that you have the capacity to wake up earlier and get housework done before it's actually time for you to officially clock in and switch on your computer for the day, then that's great! The reason why this is mentioned is to avoid falling into the potential procrastination pit by using housework that needs doing as an excuse or a crutch to prevent you from doing what is actually part of your official work day.

Effective Time Management

Using your time wisely is a skill that everyone is able to develop, focusing on getting the job done, rather than fluffing and folding laundry when you should be adding the finishing touches to a business presentation! Whether you're happy to admit to it or not, the housework isn't really going anywhere, so whether you choose to do it in place of time that could be spent being productive, or during 'off' time is completely up to you.

Chapter 22:

Work Motivation

Remaining fully motivated and 'in the zone' all day can be difficult to achieve, however there are some techniques that you can incorporate into your daily schedule to keep you motivated even though you're physically working away from a team and in total isolation from the rest of the world. This has the potential to leave you feeling vulnerable and can occasionally lead to feelings of loneliness and isolation as we've discussed before.

Staying Motivated

There are a number of ways to ensure you can become motivated and stay there through most of the day. Much of this motivation begins within yourself. You need to want to succeed badly enough to be willing to get out of bed in the morning in the right frame of mind and ready to bring your very best to your workspace every day.

I personally like getting up early, before anyone else in the home, and making use of this 'golden hour' to plough through as much as I possibly can without distractions. I enjoy the silence and solitude that this time brings.

There are a number of other ways to help keep you motivated throughout the day, some of these are:

Using Music

For some, music can be a great motivation: having your favorite band's greatest hits playing in the background can help you focus and generate creative ideas. For some, this even increases the rhythm and speed that they are able to work at, but a word of caution here would be to ensure that the music is playing in the background and not so loud that you cannot hear your own thoughts.

When it comes to music in the background, remember to keep things professional when teleconferencing with clients, colleagues or management as this would certainly NOT be an appropriate time to be streaming music.

Drawing up a Schedule

Set up your work schedule: for me, this means creating a task list of everything that needs to be done before I finish work each day or making a list of at least 5 critical things that I need to achieve the next day. Many successful business professionals recommend this as an effective strategy because it allows your subconscious to work on tasks and problems you need to manage while you are sleeping. Have you ever gone to bed the night before with some pressing issue on your mind and woken up having an 'Aha!' moment? That's exactly what I'm talking about.

Sticking to Your Work Schedule

Designing and sticking to a work schedule with key points that need to be accomplished is a great way to keep both motivated and on track with tasks that need to be completed over a set period of time. As these tasks are completed, physically cross them off the list, this will give you a sense of accomplishment and provide you with further motivation to work towards achieving the business goals you set yourself. The emphasis here should be on key points. Setting up this schedule shouldn't take you longer than 10-minutes a day. All you're trying to achieve with this schedule is a key breakdown of tasks that need to be done for the day.

Operate with a To Do List

Start your day by beginning on your list of things to do, beginning with those items that have the highest levels of priority and then working your way down. It's important to work towards achieving a goal each day and not settling for being mediocre in the quality of work that you produce.

Strive for excellence in absolutely everything that you aim to get done throughout the day. To be successful in working from home, you need to be able to prove your worth to those who have entrusted you with the job that you're currently doing. You have a choice to either give it everything you have and gain a reputation for being trustworthy, reliable and being able to pay attention to detail, or, you be labelled as someone who's merely along for the ride! The choice is always yours.

Reading or Listening to Motivational Material

You can increase your daily motivation by reading from good motivational books each day. If you're not much of a reader, aim to dedicate 30 minutes of your time to listening to a good audiobook. We have an incredible amount of knowledge available at our fingertips: this can either be ignored or used to benefit us and enhance our personal development. Successful individuals recognize that they need to keep motivated daily, and they take this responsibility on themselves to ensure that it happens.

Collect Motivational Quotes or Material

Other ways to keep motivated is by gathering motivational quotations and changing these out every day. These quotes can be found online under almost any topic you could possibly imagine. It's easy enough to choose a new quote each week and write it on Post-it notes close to your computer screen as a reminder to keep yourself motivated throughout the week.

Chapter 23:

Early Bird or Night Owl?

In his work *Hamlet*, Shakespeare has the character Polonius say "To thine own self be true" (1599). This should be considered when working remotely from your home office. We each function differently: some people are awake at the crack of dawn and find that this is the best time for them to be super-productive. They stick to the philosophy that the early bird catches the worm and prefer the quiet that working in the early hours can offer them.

Believe it or not, you can also find these individuals in physical offices, it's not just a characteristic that's exclusive to those working from home (although having a home office definitely makes it way more convenient). In a corporate environment, these are usually the individuals who'd be awake at 4:00am to avoid the daily traffic in their commute to the office. They'd usually get in several hours before anyone else and will have already processed emails and a dozen other menial tasks long before the first of their colleagues walks into the office.

Work From Home Flexibility

Working from home provides you with the unique opportunity and flexibility of being able to analyze whether you're more productive early in the morning or late at night, and then tailoring your day around these times. Synchronize your peak productivity with your work so that you can ensure that you're always producing your best work and that you get the maximum out of your day.

Best of Both Worlds

For me, I have the best of both worlds because I'm working over three different time zones. While this can be beneficial, it can also bring with it an entirely new set of challenges and problems. In the event that you're like me and work between the UK, India and the USA, make sure that you respect the time zones that your colleagues are working in. Be considerate of their time and avoid sending documentation or emails when you know that they're not available. Sending out emails at 2:00am to ask for some clarification on a spreadsheet that's only required for a meeting at the end of the week may not be the best way to develop solid working relationships with others.

This is where applications like Slack are perfect, as they allow you to set your own availability times, ensuring that even if your communication is submitted to a colleague in another time zone, they will only receive your request once they log in or become available.

Consider Your Family

Working unreasonable hours could also have a negative impact on the people within your own home. Some individuals are light sleepers and if you're going back and forwards to the kitchen all night to make coffee or grab a quick bite to eat, this may disturb and disrupt their sleep patterns. This could place unnecessary strain on family relationships. If you are the insomniac that works into the wee hours of the morning because you find that's when you're most productive, be considerate of other family members and maybe ensure that your workspace is as far away from the rest of the family as possible.

It may be a good idea to consider creating your workspace within the basement or a loft that was once used for storage; that way you would be less likely to have miserable looking faces every morning due to disturbed sleep.

The reality of working remotely is that you can schedule your own working hours, however these should be realistic and try to accommodate everyone as far as you possibly can.

Chapter 24:

Friends Without Work

Benefits

While it's important to maintain healthy relationships with others to avoid going stir crazy from loneliness, it's also vital to communicate to friends, neighbors and loved ones that you are actually working from home. This means that you need to be able to remain focused and disciplined to get the job done. Let them know that dropping by unannounced while you're in the middle of a business meeting or an important negotiation is just not on, as it breaks your concentration and robs you of valuable time: time when you should be productive, and time that you are actually being paid to do work in.

Clearly Communicate Boundaries

Being forced to break your concentration, especially when you're 'in the zone' or deep in the middle of a project, is going to set you back with precious time that you can never recover. Often when you're in this state of mind, your thought processes are running way ahead of you, and once these patterns have been disrupted, unless you've captured whatever you were thinking about on paper, these ideas may be difficult to recall and get back again. It also means that you will need to sacrifice time from elsewhere to catch up at some point. Make it clear to everybody in your circle when it's appropriate to call or visit.

Dodge Private Phone Calls

While people may believe that their phone call is going to be a brief one, these can often lead to in-depth and distracting catch-ups that often prove to be lengthy and can be as bad as physically having people in the room with you. There are several ways to avoid these disruptions from stealing away valuable time:

- Make it clear to them that you are actually working from home and that your work needs to come first at all times.
- Set boundaries regarding calls or visits. You can schedule these for outside of office hours and be firm and clear as to when these are.
- Something that works well for me is to turn my phone on 'silent.' I schedule time during the day

to physically check that nobody needs me urgently, but by doing so, I avoid unnecessary disruptions that interfere with quality work time. Earlier we discussed having a dedicated work line or work phone that's specifically for business purposes. This number should always be on during your working hours: this will ensure that you don't miss out on anything that's vitally important when it comes to work.

- Personal calls should be directed to your personal number and answered outside of work hours or during breaks. This includes instant messaging, social media and anything else that can interrupt effective business.

- By setting strict work / home / social boundaries, you are able to separate these from each other more effectively and prove your loyalty to those who have hired you to complete work for them in the first place. There's nothing more appreciated by employers than having employees prioritize the things that they've been tasked to do.

- Explain to friends and family members who expect you to be available 24/7 that if they drop in unexpectedly when you're in the middle of something that's work related, you can't really pay them the full quality attention that they truly deserve as loved ones.

- When working with children in your home, make sure that your office is separated as far away from their play area or bedrooms as possible. This is not only to avoid noise disruption, but also distractions that can be just as challenging as uninvited guests. The last thing that you need is to be pressurized by sibling rivalry in the background of a video conference or important business call.

Avoid Other Disruptions

Make these decisions regarding disruptions during work hours right from the start so that there's an agreement in place and everyone is onboard with the rules. This can be challenging when you have smaller children at home, and they don't always understand that Mommy or Daddy can't play with them right now. For older kids, it may take putting a sign on the door that lets them know that you're busy and can't be disturbed right now.

Working from home will never prove to be 100% free of disruptions: the friendly courier guy is dropping off some important documents that you need to sign for, a pet needs to urgently get to the vet, or one of the children requires the attention of a doctor or dentist.

There's no perfect formula out there, what this chapter is trying to communicate is how to minimize these as far as possible so that your day can still be productive and you don't find yourself working unpaid overtime trying to play 'catch up' because someone never got the memo that working from home actually requires work!

Photo Credit - JacLou DL from Pixabay

Chapter 25:

Mental Health

As individuals, we are each unique, with a different set of strengths and weaknesses that allow us to get through each day. While working from home may present as an ideal solution to some, it may cause feelings of anxiety and stress in others. There's no real right or wrong answer as to whether or not it's good or bad for your mental health, as there are arguments that may be heard and supported on both sides.

Feeling Isolated and Alone

For some, working from home could leave them feeling isolated and completely disconnected from the rest of the world, mainly due to the lack of regular contact with people. In an office environment, it's easy to operate effectively if you're an extrovert and you feel that you need constant reinforcement from others to let you know that you're actually doing okay.

While this doesn't just boil down to whether you're an introvert or an extrovert, it also speaks to the state of your mental health and how you connect with people in general. Many individuals thrive on the 'buzz' that an office environment creates. Even those with poor social skills still benefit from having others around them.

Stuck in the Same Environment

Working from home forces you to be in the same environment constantly, which can in turn lead to symptoms of being trapped within the same walls. This is part of the reason why it's so important to take regular breaks and make sure that you take every opportunity to get out and away from your workspace wherever possible.

There's often a misconception surrounding those who work remotely: that they have it so much easier than those who commute and report into an office daily, physically clocking in and clocking out. Working from home is not always clearly understood by those 'office colleagues.' They believe that working from home can be a dream, lounging around in your PJ's all day while answering a few emails from your dining room table.

Two Opinions about Working From Home

There are two distinct camps when it comes to remote work and mental health. These are outlined as follows:

- For many, the time spent commuting to the office is totally wasted and they'd much rather focus the time and energy that they save commuting on things that are really important to them.
- They prefer the freedom of working 'unshackled' from a stiff, formal environment where they have a manager breathing down their necks most of the time, expecting them to account for every second within a day.
- They actually become more efficient and productive working remotely because they can focus intently on what needs to be done.
- They're also not in an environment where they can become easily distracted by co-workers dropping by their office or cubicle to have a quick chat about something that's completely irrelevant to their work, or getting pulled into meetings that run well over time and have no real value because the agenda is rehashed over

and over again, and nobody is willing to stand up to convince management that this time is totally counter-productive.

- They feel less stress and anxiety because they are in control of their time and can choose how to balance both work and life commitments.
- They no longer feel guilty about having to bring work home, because they're already working from home and can set their own parameters and boundaries. If they get through whatever they need to do at a quicker pace, the time saved can be allocated to more important things.
- These individuals feel in control of their time, their day and their lives. They're also in control of their level of productivity, and this directly influences their self-esteem and self-confidence.
- They know what needs to be done and get down to doing it. Most of these individuals are able to manage their time effectively and don't rely on the direct feedback or input from management to confirm that they are valuable within the organization.

On the other side, those who desperately need to feel connected with people can struggle with working remotely in the following ways:

- These individuals need to be told constantly that they are important to the success of an organization and thrive on feedback. Even negative feedback makes them feel like part of a team.
- Their commute in and out of the office provides them with human interaction that they crave. Seeing familiar faces on the subway, or in the elevator on the way to the office can make their day.
- These workers often find it necessary to stop by and have a quick chat with others in the office. They will spend longer in the kitchen making their coffee just to connect with others in the company.
- They struggle to work in an environment that's isolated because it's difficult for them to structure their time efficiently by themselves. They prefer to be told what to do, rather than being able to take the initiatives for themselves.
- They feel guilty if they're not 'working' 24/7. While that's something that is completely unrealistic and will never be required by any corporation when working remotely, these individuals believe that they need to be constantly proving themselves, and in doing so they place unnecessary and undue pressure on their daily work. This pressure can eventually

lead to stress and anxiety, which in turn can lead to depression.

It's important to weigh all the pros and cons when it comes to working remotely. You know your own needs and personality traits better than anyone. If you don't have strong emotional intelligence and the type of personality that can remain focused when working in isolation, then working from home may not be the ideal solution for you.

Chapter 26:

Sleep = Healthy Brain

Whether you're a night owl or an early bird, one of the most important habits to develop when working remotely is a healthy sleep pattern. For some, this means getting a full 8-hours of shut eye in order to function properly the next day; for others, this figure may be lower. You know your own body and how much time you really need in order to feel fully rejuvenated and revived, ready to face the challenges that each new workday brings with it.

How Much Sleep Is Enough Sleep?

The reality is that you simply cannot be effective if you don't get enough sleep. Sleep is what keeps our brains healthy and prevents us from suffering from physical, mental and emotional burnout. We need sleep to be able to concentrate effectively, and it's also vital to our wellbeing and overall health.

Lack of sleep could result in obesity and mortality rates for sleep-deprived people are also higher. There are a number of ways to assist you in getting enough uninterrupted sleep:

- Either switch your cell / mobile phone off at night time when you go to bed, or remove it from the room completely. That way you won't be tempted to check your emails when your body should be getting the rest that it needs. Remember that I spoke about a 2:00am email earlier. It's one that I not only received, but also responded to ... talk about not having things under control!
- The blue light from your phone can also have a negative chemical effect on your brain if you check your phone directly before trying to sleep.
- Avoid checking on social media posts just before falling asleep: this could have an ongoing psychological effect on your brain, causing nightmares or for your mind to go wandering in another direction rather than getting the rest and relaxation that you actually deserve.
- There are often times when you may be working on a project and you have an epiphany in the middle of the night. This could make the same thoughts play in your head over and over again. To help with this, I have a small notebook next to my bed to take notes that I

can refer to again in the morning. The brain is a remarkable organ, however, once you manage to put something down on paper, you can physically free your brain. The last thing you want is for your thought processes to get stuck, especially when you need your creative juices to flow freely. If you don't assist your brain with that, you can get stuck in an overthinking pattern, trying to process ideas that are coming at you from every angle. Write things down to help get them out of your head and avoid insomnia.

Peaceful Sleep

Key ingredients to ensure sufficient peaceful rest include:

- Curtains or blinds that make your bedroom dark enough for you to actually sleep. There's nothing worse than having a streetlight shining directly into the room, or seeing flashing lights from surrounding traffic in the neighborhood. When you get into bed, you need to be able to fall asleep as quickly as possible.

- Your room should have sufficient ventilation, to the point where it is comfortable throughout the year. You don't want it to be freezing in winter or overheated in summer. Try and keep the temperature as consistent as you can throughout the year, that way your sleep patterns can also remain constant.

- Noise pollution can also interfere and disturb sleep. Try and eliminate this as much as possible. This can be done by hanging heavier drapes over windows, keeping windows closed and avoid using air-conditioning, or even physically relocating your bedroom to a room that's furthest away from where the main sound is coming from.

- Avoid drinking anything with caffeine just before retiring for the night if you know that it's likely to interfere with trying to fall asleep.

- Make sure that you eat your evening meal several hours before going to bed, giving your body a chance to digest food. Going to sleep on a full stomach can not only give you indigestion, but it can also lead to feelings of being bloated and uncomfortable, two factors that can prevent a decent night's rest.

- When we get sufficient sleep, our creativity, productivity and level of professionalism improve drastically. Without sleep, we are less accurate and can be prone to making simple mistakes or errors in judgement during our workday.

- Avoid working where you sleep, as this can be distracting when it comes to sleep patterns. It's too easy to get an idea in the middle of the night, switch your laptop on and physically continue working when you should be resting. This is why it's important to allocate a separate work area that's away from your bedroom. Your bedroom should be a sanctuary where you can gain some much-needed rest and relaxation.

- When it comes to working from your bed, laptops have small fans that can potentially overheat when they are not on a flat, hard surface. Working with your laptop on a duvet prevents this air from circulating properly and can potentially lead to your system overheating.

Chapter 27:

All or Nothing

This balancing act of working from a home-based office doesn't mean that you're chained to a desk permanently. We've spoken about some healthy ways in which you can remain connected with the office and your colleagues by scheduling times that are convenient for you to go into the office. For some, this may be going to the office at least twice a week, while for others, this may only need to happen every second month or for senior executive meetings on a monthly basis.

The most important thing when getting this balance correct is to ensure that it's comfortable, you're managing to get through all of the work assigned to you, you're producing results and you are still feeling connected with the rest of the team.

Working remotely can either be a short-term solution, for example while recovering from a surgery that requires you to take things easy for several months, or it can be a permanent decision, but regardless, it's something that needs to work for not only you but for all parties concerned.

Tri-Win Formula

If you think in terms of a triangle, with each vertex or point representing three entities: one of these is you as an individual and your career, the second is the organization that you're representing and the third is your home and family. You need to get to a point where there's a three-point 'win'. If any one of these entities is in a 'losing' position, you have lost the main goal or reason why you wanted to work remotely in the first place.

Analyze which one of these three areas is lacking, and then devise a workable action plan to restore a three-way balance where everyone is back in the winning seat. For example, you may need to renegotiate your working hours, either with your employer, or with your family. This may mean going back to square one and designing a strategy that's workable, where you actually get everything that you want out of the deal, but where it's not at the expense of your employer, your family or yourself.

There's no point in constantly feeling like you are part of a juggling act, with too many balls in the air simultaneously, and you simply can't cope. That's not winning! Your workload needs to be realistic and doable. You need to be motivated to physically do everything necessary to reach targets, deadlines or other company projects assigned to you. If you are feeling overwhelmed, speak to someone in authority about it: open lines of communication are always better than simply ignoring the problems and hoping that all the things you're unhappy about are going to magically disappear.

Check in with your direct manager on a regular basis to find out how you're doing. Ask them to be straight up with you: if there are areas that you need to be improving on, ask for leadership, guidance, mentorship, or possible training options available that can help you improve and meet the standards that they require. This should almost always be on the agenda for one-on-one meetings with your immediate manager. Feedback on our performance is one of the ways in which we can improve. It's also better to ask for this feedback sooner rather than later. Employers always have their hands full with many other members of staff, and it's important to remember that none of them are mind readers. They cannot know what you're thinking unless you actually communicate with them.

How does each member of your family feel about you working from home? Is it actually strengthening your relationships, or is it breaking them down? Are they seeing more of you now that you're around, or are you so consumed by work all the time that you're struggling to find the 'off switch?' Are your main reasons for wanting to work from home in the first place still valid? Are you organized enough to physically separate work and family and create a better balance between the two? Are you able to prioritize between the two, and make effective use of the time that you would have spent commuting to the office, building family relationships instead? Is your physical mood more agreeable since coming home, or are you constantly flustered and under pressure because of work requirements to the point where your family is afraid 'to poke the bear'?

If any of these are out of synch or harmony, it's time to re-evaluate what's important in the long run. What's going to win? There will come a time when this re-evaluation is necessary. It's part of our natural path of progression. As children grow older, priorities change, companies have different needs and individual career aspirations and goals change. Continue assessing each of these areas to ensure that you're still on the right track when it comes to what you want to achieve from life.

Without this, there can be no work / life balance and harmony.

Chapter 28:

SMART Goal Setting

Getting tasks completed on time and managing objectives effectively requires planning, dedication and commitment. They also ideally necessitate working on projects with clearly defined goals. While there are several variations on goal setting, I'd like to focus on the one that I favor most of all—SMART Goals. One of the most important things to remember when it comes to goal setting is that your goals need to be in writing. If you don't write them down, you will never do anything to work towards them, because they will be merely dreams in your head.

One of the best ways to do this is to work from A6 cards that have each goal clearly outlined and defined. These should then be placed where they are highly visible throughout the day, so that you can be reminded of what you deem to be important to you. Another reason to have them on A6 cards is that they're easy to carry in your wallet or diary, somewhere that you can review them daily.

Create a daily ritual where you set aside some time to go through each of your goals at least three times a day.

You can do this morning, noon and night, or alternately, three times directly after one another.

By the end of this process, you'll be astonished as to how quickly and easily your goals will suddenly begin to become realized. The right doors will be opened for you, you'll manage to complete that training course in record time with great results. Everything that you've ever wanted will slowly begin falling into place, if you want it hard enough and are prepared to follow the steps and process as outlined below.

The word SMART is actually an acronym for the following:

Specific

Each goal that you choose to focus on must be clearly outlined in writing where there can be nothing that could be misinterpreted. It's cutting through all the red tape and getting straight to the point with what you actually want to achieve.

In order to be specific in setting clearly defined goals, you need to know exactly what it is that you want. This can usually be done by asking yourself simple questions based on the 6-W and 1-H formula. This formula can be applied to almost any subject to help you clarify and fine tune your goals: before you make the first move towards achieving them, you must have a crystal clear picture in your mind of exactly what it is that you want.

You can ask yourself the following questions: Who? What? When? Where? Why? Who? And How? Once you have managed to find the answers to each of the above, you should have a much better idea of exactly what it is that you're after. In other words, you will have a picture that is specific.

Measurable

For a goal to be measurable, there should be sufficient parameters or guidelines in place that allow you to measure your level of performance. It's being able to constantly check yourself and your performance off against standards that are measurable and quantifiable. This may require breaking down a massive project or goal into bite-size chunks to ensure that you can mark off where you are succeeding, but it could also help highlight shortcomings and areas where more effort needs to be put in.

When considering how to measure a goal, some of the questions that you should be asking yourself should be:

How Much? How Often? By When? And occasionally even Why? By asking these questions, you are able to quantify your goals and refine them even further.

Achievable

For any goal to be successfully completed, it needs to be realistic and achievable. Anything less than this will cause you to lose focus or interest in working towards completing it. An achievable goal is one you believe that you can achieve within the time allotted. This is applicable to anything, whether you're working on personal goals or combined goals as an organization. You will only work hard at something when you believe that it's doable. Ask yourself:

- Is what I'm aiming for realistic?
- Is this really what I want to achieve for myself?
- Who am I doing this for?

Relevant

Is the goal or set of goals applicable to the work that you're doing, or are they going to add value to your life?

Many people work on other people's goals for them, and wonder why they are frustrated with where they currently are in life. If you aren't genuinely passionate about something that you're working on, give it a miss and find something else that will set your life aflame.

Some questions to ask at this point should be:

- Why is this important to me?
- How am I going to feel when I achieve this?
- How are others going to react towards me if I achieve this?
- Am I doing this to please myself or someone else? (if the answer to this question is to please someone else, then please reconsider the goal).

Time-bound

The final part of the SMART acronym is that each goal needs to have a deadline: a time frame that you're prepared to give yourself in order to achieve it. Without placing a deadline on a goal or dream, it's pretty much just wishful thinking and you'll find yourself becoming frustrated. You'll struggle to find the actual motivation to ever achieve any of your hopes, dreams or desires.

Break your goal down into smaller, manageable steps or pieces that you can achieve over a realistic period of time and then work towards achieving each step. There's no goal that's worth having that you don't need to actually work towards. Very few people are handed everything that they want out of life on a silver platter without having to lift a finger.

Work systematically and in a disciplined manner to achieve each of the SMART goals that you set for yourself. Don't be too hard on yourself, but also don't be prepared to give up too easily. There are reasons why certain individuals achieve more out of life than others, and one of these reasons is definitely effective goal setting.

The SMART method of goal setting has been around for many decades, with the first instance of this technique of goal setting being attributed to Peter Drucker in his book *Management By Objectives* (1954). Things snowballed from there with other attributions being made to individuals like George T. Doran for *Management Review*, (1981), Professor Robert S. Rubin from Saint Louis University, and even Paul J. Meyer, the founder of Success Motivation International who describes SMART goal setting in his book *Attitude is Everything: If You Want to Succeed Above and Beyond* (2003).

Chapter 29:

Pets - Help or Hindrance

Having pets around can be a great way to boost your morale and break some of the monotony and isolation that can creep in when you're working from your home office. They've also been known to relieve stress and ease tension and anxiety. In this instance it's a case of choosing your pets wisely and ensuring that they don't get out of control, especially when it comes to behaving in a professional manner during business hours.

Whether you're a dog person or a cat person, having either pet around the house can come with its own set of challenges. Make sure that your work and even work equipment is protected at all times from your beloved pets.

Photo Credit - Ruca Suza from Pexels

All about Puppies

Puppies love chewing on things and can easily destroy anything from the wheels of your office chair to any boxes of files that you may have stacked on your office floor. They are easily bored and can become frustrated, which is why having them in your office space really isn't the best idea in the first place. If you feel that you can't live without them, make certain that they have sufficient quiet chew toys available to keep themselves entertained, away from anything that's work related.

Dogs are prone to barking, which can be disruptive and distracting if you are in the middle of a conference call with a colleague or client.

When I first started working from home, in the middle of one of these conference calls my dog was snoring so loudly under the desk that the person on the other side of the call asked me what was making the noise in the background: talk about an embarrassing situation! I'm sure they believed that I had nodded off during our conversation! I quickly learned that as much as I loved my dog, my workspace needed to have certain boundaries put in place that excluded allowing my pets into this inner sanctum.

Dogs can also be noisy when barking outside your office window. This is one of the reasons for making wise decisions and taking all factors into consideration when choosing where and how you're going to set up your home office.

Decoy Desk Accessories

I once saw a guy actually placing a 'decoy' dummy keyboard on his desk because his cat loved running over the keyboard. This can wreak absolute havoc on your work, especially if you need to move away from your desk for a few minutes. You also need to avoid muddy pawprints on official company documents if your cat decides to wander outside just after it's rained and brings mud back into the house.

Protect your work area at all costs, whether this means closing this area off entirely so that it becomes a 'no pet zone,' or finding other ways to make sure that your equipment is safe at all times.

Make 'Pet Time'

Pets can be a great way to relieve stress when you need to have a break from your work. You can do this by spending quality time with them when you do need to take a routine break. Take them outside and play with them, or go for a jog or a walk.

In many ways, pets are similar to other members of your family, you need to let them know that they're important to you, but there's a time and a place for everything. Try and minimize the number of disruptions caused by your furry family members.

Keeping Pets Out!

What do you do if you don't have an office that's in an enclosed space where you can physically close the door to keep your pets out? There are a number of ways to minimize the negative effects of having your pets sharing the same space as you: after all, they are part of the family and just because you're now working from home, it doesn't mean that they have to go in order to make you more effective at your job.

Some of these ideas include:

- Create a feeding station to avoid having to get up and feed your dog or cat throughout the day, making sure that they have food and water before you even begin your workday. This way you don't need to worry about breaking your stride while working to get up to give them food or water.
- Create a safe space under your desk for your pet: ensure the area beneath your desk is completely free from anything that can become a substitute chew toy. Both dogs and cats love to curl up at the feet of their owners, especially if this space is warm and sunny. Create this kind of space for them so they know they are

welcome but establish boundaries. If they are going to be there for extended periods of time, make sure that they have the means to get out of the room, or take them out whenever you're going for your own breaks.

- Exercise with your dog before work: create an early morning routine where you and your dog go for a run. Feed them once you get back home. As this becomes a habit, you'll notice that your dog will most likely settle for a nap, allowing you to get on with your day with few interruptions. You need to do everything in your power to prevent them from feeling bored, because this is when pets act out. By exercising your dog both morning and night, you will both get the much-needed exercise that you deserve and spend quality time together. You'll be able to keep in excellent shape, and let your pet know that you still have time for them.

While having pets can be distracting, they can also be a sense of comfort when working remotely because they can help remove feelings of being physically isolated from others. The most important thing is making sure that whatever pet you have feels wanted and loved, and this may mean taking a few minutes out of your busy schedule acknowledging them, without rewarding bad behavior. If your cat keeps on walking across your keyboard, find a way to deter them from this behavior:

it may mean going the 'fake keyboard' route as mentioned above.

If it's difficult getting your pets under control in the space you're working from, you may need to re-think your strategy and opt for a goldfish somewhere in your office instead. Some of them have unique personalities and can be just as relaxing to be around as a furry companion.

Chapter 30:

Relationships - Children

and Family

One of the main reasons for choosing to work remotely is usually for the benefit of children and family. It's wanting to spend more quality time with them, being able to dedicate the time that you would have spent commuting to and from work to them, rather than wasting those hours away. If you've chosen to work from home in order to be closer to your children and family, then make sure that you actually do it.

Take time out every day to give your family some of the time that you've saved. Spend the time with them and use it to strengthen your relationship with them, rather than shutting them out using 'work' as an excuse.

Establish Family Ground Rules

Just as you set up boundaries for your pets to keep your work environment safe while you're working, you may need to set some ground rules when it comes to your children and family. They need to understand that during certain hours you're not available to them due to the fact that you have work to do. However, your work should never get to the point where it becomes all-consuming and addictive, and there's no room for your family. If that's the case, you might as well be working from an actual office every day.

When I chose to make the transition to working from home, my children understood straight away that they needed to leave me alone when I was working, after all it's all for them. They got the fact that if I was in the middle of a meeting I wasn't to be interrupted. However, you need to get the dynamics of this work / life balance correct when it comes to relationships with your children and your family.

Support Family in Family Events

Make time to support events that are important to your family members, and let them know that you're there for them by actively listening to them. This applies to all members of your family. If they're on-board with you and understand that they are the reason behind certain sacrifices, they will respect your 'work time' more and leave you to be productive whenever you need to be.

Photo Credit - wokandpix from Pixabay

Support your children by being there for them for important events in their lives. After all, this is the reason for choosing to work from home in the first place (or at least it has been for me). Attend school events like sports and plays: these are the moments that they will remember for the rest of their lives. They'll appreciate that you were there for them and that you took the time out to show that you care. Remember that I stated right at the beginning of this book that my main reason for choosing to work remotely was solely driven out of the number of things I'd already missed out on with my children.

Be 100% Present

Be there for them whenever they need you and be 100% present in the moment. If you need to sacrifice a time when you should have been working (in order to attend a school event), ensure that this time is caught up by sacrificing a lunch hour or other breaks to stay on top of your work.

You can strengthen ties and relationships by spending quality time with loved ones. It's not always the amount of time, but what you do with the time that you have together. Learn to leave work matters aside when you're out with your family. Leave the work phone at home: your office will survive for a few hours without you. Use this time with your family wisely and be fully engaged. It's easy to sense when someone has other things on their minds, rather than having their full, undivided attention on you.

Eat Together as a Family

Another suggestion when it comes to strengthening your family is to set aside mealtimes and eat together as a family, without mobile phones. This can be easily achieved by placing everyone's phones and devices into a basket before sitting down together as a family for an evening meal. Use this time to really communicate effectively with one another and to discuss each other's day, or anything else that's really important.

Technology absorbs so much of our time nowadays that being able to physically connect with others where you are 100% fully engaged can be extremely challenging. By making a small adjustment in your home, you'll learn more about what's really going on in everybody's lives pretty quickly. It will also add to the amount of quality time that you get to spend with one another. Another healthy rule when it comes to eating dinner together at the dinner table is that nobody gets to leave until the last person is done eating, and that everybody shares in the responsibility to clear away the dishes and tidy up the kitchen.

If you happen to have sacrificed some of your work time to spend quality time with your family, you may need to return to your office to play catch up for an hour or so: believe me, this time will be well worth the time devoted to your children and your family. There's a quote that's attributed to Paul Tsongas (1941-1997) that says, "No one on his deathbed ever said, I wish I had spent more time on my business."

Choosing how you divide and devote quality time to your family is probably one of the most important decisions you'll ever get to make in this life.

Chapter 31:

Sickness and Vacations

Illness

People working remotely from home usually take fewer sick days purely because they're not exposed to as many germs and infections as they would be if working from an office. That's not to say that people at home are totally immune to becoming ill. Especially for workers who have children going to school, the risk of them bringing contagions into the home are just as great.

The most important protocol that needs to be followed when you're feeling sick is to notify the office, teams, or clients that you're unavailable due to illness. This is something that's easy enough to do on instant messaging, or you can set up an 'out of office' notification on your email account.

Taking the time required to rest and recover completely is extremely important and not only in your best interest, but in the best interest of your company as a whole. We all know that, when you're not feeling great, it can be difficult to focus and concentrate properly, and this is when errors happen. The last thing you need is to make a huge mistake because you're on a medication that makes you feel drowsy and you're choosing to ignore the advice of your physician to take it easy. There are way too many people out there who feel 'fine' after a day or so and decide to return to work too soon, only to relapse with more serious conditions that take longer to overcome. Be sensible about your health and don't second guess what your medical professional has advised you to do.

It can be especially tempting for a workaholic to grab their laptop and try and push through the day while working from their bed, but the truth is that if and when you're booked off for bed rest, there's a good reason for it, and the last thing you need is to physically crash and burn because you're stubborn.

Only return to work once you're feeling better and you know that you've received the all clear from your doctor to do so. This is for your own benefit, but also protects the reputation of the organization that you're working for. There's no point in trying to tough it out and push yourself to keep going despite feeling like death warmed up! There aren't any awards for being stubborn. Remember that you're human and we can all suffer from illnesses that can wipe us out and knock us flat on our backs. The sooner you get correctly diagnosed and medicated, the sooner you get onto the path to a full recovery.

Vacation Days

Sometimes it can be difficult for office-bound colleagues to accept that those who work from home are actually 'working'. Maybe it's because they don't physically see you in the office or at your workstation, and therefore assume that you're kicking back and chilling at home in your sweats living a glorious life and simply picking up a paycheck at the end of each month!

In a lot of instances, those working from home can actually spend much more time working, in terms of 'actual work hours', than their office bound counterparts. As such, when working from a home office, you are entitled to as many vacation days as anybody else, as stipulated in your contract, and these vacation days should be taken without feeling guilty about it.

When you've decided on your vacation calendar and once it's been approved by management, HR or whoever else needs to sign this off for you, communicate this information to anyone and everyone who could possibly be looking for you during this time.

This is yet another benefit that comes into play when having two landlines in your home, a personal one and one that's dedicated to work. When on vacation, leave a voice message on your business landline providing clarity as to dates when you'll be in and out of the office. You may need to provide emergency contact details for others working with you who will be available while you are off.

Make it clear on shared calendars on Trello or Slack as to when you are planning to be away, and when you will return to work. Even if you aren't planning to physically take a vacation away from your home, everyone needs sufficient down time in order to rejuvenate and recharge for the next wave of work.

Gratitude

Be thankful for this opportunity and for being able to work from home: there are many people out there who simply do not have this option. You should be thankful and show gratitude to the teams you work with: be mindful to thank them during meetings, instant messaging and emails, where appropriate. Give people that report to you their moment to shine, leave the ladder down and help people grow. In my experience working relationships always work better if you show you are grateful for people's hard work, and if you show them they are valued, because they are an extension of your own work.

Burnout

For those working from home offices, or working remotely, burnout is something that's all too common. If proper boundaries, hours, breaks, and limitations are not set from the very beginning, it becomes too easy to get trapped in a work cycle that far exceeds and outweighs the actual number of hours required to be worked in a day. Most individuals working from home will admit to the fact that they:

- Check their emails when they're supposed to be off the clock.
- Reply or respond to the emails when they're supposed to be off the clock.
- Help a colleague out even when they're supposed to be on leave.
- Assist with something that a colleague needs done, outside of office hours.

Finding a balance between work and life can often prove to be tricky, especially when it comes to starting to work remotely. You want to be able to impress those that you report to, and what better way to do that than to do your job to the very best of your ability? Remember that those who oversee you are also human. They've tasked you with certain assignments and are relying on you to make things happen, however they aren't looking for Superman or Wonder Woman! They want someone who they know they can trust and rely on. You are absolutely no use to them if you are totally frazzled and burned out due to unnecessary pressure and stress that you may be putting on yourself.

STOP, re-evaluate what it is that you need to be doing and get your head back in the game realistically. Do what you know you can do, rest when you need to rest by clocking out at the end of the day, and take leave as and when it's due to you.

Conclusion

Having discussed so many different reasons to consider when working from a home-based office and whether working at home is better than working in a big office, in conclusion there are a number of important considerations you need to make.

First of all, reframe and clarify your main reason for working from home in the first place. For me, it's definitely been to spend more time with my family and loved ones and despite all the challenges and changes in my life, my family relationships are stronger than ever before. If this is your reason for working from home, make the most of every second spent together with your children and loved ones. This time passes by all too quickly, and as we've mentioned, time is something that's finite. Once it's gone, you can never get it back again. Embrace every activity that you're able to share with your family, and create memories that will stand the test of time. Children grow up so quickly and there will come a time when they'd much rather be hanging out with their friends than their parents. Cherish the moments that you get to share with them and record these somewhere that can be accessed whenever you want.

Be grateful that you've been able to spend quality time with your children and loved ones while you've been able to work from home. There is no amount of money that can ever buy this time, so enjoy it while it lasts. Maximize every minute in the day where you've been able to eat breakfast, lunch, and dinner together as a family—there aren't very many people on the planet who can claim that privilege. Due to school commitments, and work commitments, this may not happen every day—when it does though, be grateful for the time that you get to be together.

You should also recognize the financial benefits attached to working from home and using this money wisely: that's another key to running a successful business from home. Take the money that you would have spent commuting to and from the office daily and set it aside into a savings account, an investment portfolio, or a college account for your children. Depending on how far you would normally have to commute daily to physically work, factor in not only the fuel that you would have spent travelling to and from the office, but also wear and tear on your vehicle, parking costs, toll fees and other expenses; in other words, factor in everything. This is the monthly amount of money you need to set aside because in reality. Separate funds from the above finances if you do need to go into the office or out to meet with clients, although this should be expensed out separately and picked up by your employer. This may mean negotiating these costs up front before you begin working from your home office.

Be grateful for the way that your life has improved now that you have the freedom to work from home rather than the office. While you may still feel some of the pressure of having to deliver on tasks and projects, there's definitely no longer footfall from colleagues stopping by your office to 'chat' about random stuff that robs you of time that could be spent being productive.

List all the benefits or ways that your home / work / life / balance has improved as a result of the incredible gift that you've been entrusted with: working from home. One of the best ways to repay the employer that has given you this gift is by showing up every single day and making sure that you're ready to perform and do whatever it takes to meet any and all targets, tasks and commitments entrusted to you.

Working from home is seldom monitored closely, which can easily provide you with the opportunity of not doing what's required of you. You have the choice of physically doing the job assigned to you to the best of your ability, or merely skating through with something that's half-hearted or mediocre. Unfortunately, most large corporations don't do mediocre very well and going down this route will only lead to in-depth scrutiny by management and a breakdown in any trust that they may have had in you before. You're sure to have to face performance reviews from time to time, and I can guarantee that these aren't going to go very well if you're not delivering on the mandate that the company has given you. In short, mediocrity isn't really an option if you want to continue working from home.

Prove yourself right from the start and continue striving for excellence everyday thereafter: this is what has worked for me and resulted in a number of promotions!

Is it easy? No! It's work ... but at the end of the day, that's what you've been hired to do. By putting your best foot forward every time you step into your home-based office and log into your actual account, you're sending a message to those who agreed to you working remotely in the first place, that they weren't wrong about you. You're proving your worth to the company and you're showing them that you have integrity and can be trusted, two qualities that aren't all that common anymore and will serve you well in your career.

References

(2016). 5 Time Management Tips for Working from Home. https://www.theworkathomewoman.com/time-management-tips/

(2019). How to Stay Sane When Working From Home With Kids. https://thewirecutter.com/blog/how-to-stay-sane-when-working-from-home-with-children/

12 Powerful Business Benefits of VoIP (Don't Miss This). https://blog.panterranetworks.com/business-benefits-of-voip

Agrawal, A. J. (n.d.). 7 Tips For Staying Productive At Your Home Office With A Pet. https://www.inc.com/aj-afrawal/7-tips-for-staying-productive-at-your-home-office-with-a-pet.html

Cyprus, J. (2017). 8 Strategies for Staying on Top of Housework While Working from Home. https://5minutesformom.com/126000/housework-while-working-from-home/

Dinardi, Gaetano. (n.d.). 32 Working from Home Tips You Can Do Right Now (Updated). https://nextiva.com/blog/working-from-home-tips.html

Drucker, P. (1954). The Practice of Management. New York: Harper.

Forleo, M. (2016). 8 Tips To Overcome Loneliness When Working From Home. https://www.mariaforleo.com/2016/11/online-isolation/

Foroux, D. (n.d.). What Is Procrastination? Why We Do It & How To Stop. https://dariusforoux.com/what-is-procrastination/

Johnson, C. (n.d.). 20 Reasons to Let Your Employees Work From Home. https://www.entrepreneur.com/article/253896

Lilyquist, M. (2019). 9 Reasons Why You Should Work From Home. https://www.thebalancesmb.com/should-i-work-from-home-10-reasons-you-should-1794195

Marikar, S. (2015). 8 Apps That Will Revolutionize How You Work From Home.

https://www.inc.com/magazine/201512/sheila-marikar/essential-tech-tools-and-apps-for-your-remote-team.html

Matthews, K. (n.d.). Easy Time Management Techniques for Remote Workers. https://facilethings.com/blog/en/easy-time-management-techniques-for-remote-workers

Meyer, P. J. (2003) Attitude is Everything: If You Want to Succeed Above and Beyond. English: Paul J. Meyer Resources.

Milovanovic, K. (n.d.). 4 Easy Ways to Avoid Procrastination When Working From Home. https://www.lifehack.org/468575/4-easy-ways-to-avoid-procrastination-when-working-from-home

Moran, G. (2020). How To maintain your mental health while working from home. https://fastcompany.com/90479504/how-to-maintain-your-mental-health-while-working-from-home

O'Toole, K. (2012). Researchers: Flexibility May Be the Key to Increased Productivity. https://www.gsb.stanford.edu/insights/researchers-flexibility-may-be-key-increased-productivity

Pinola, M. (2020). The 7 biggest remote work challenges (and how to overcome them). https://zapier.com/blog/remote-work-challenges/

Presson, L. (n.d.). Working From Home? 4 Times You Should Sign Off. https://themuse.com/amp/advice/working-from-home-4-times-you-should-sign-off

Sawa, D. B. (2019). Extreme loneliness or the perfect balance? How to work from home and stay healthy. https://theguardian.com/lifeandstyle/2019/mar/25/extreme-loneliness-or-the-perfect-balance-how-to-work-from-home-and-stay-healthy

Schwartz, J. (2017). Time Management & Working From Home. https://www.medium.com/jyssicaschwartz/time-management-working-from-home-9e9a548a766

Smith, P., (2020). Working From Home Might Take A Toll On Your Mental Health. https://www.huffpost.com/entry/working-from-home-mental-health_n_5afd88e2e4b0a59b4e014602

Tsongas, P. (1941-1997) Paul Tsongas Quotes. https://www.brainyquote.com/

Withers, N. (2015). 12 Tips to Stay Healthy When Working From Home. https://www.entrepreneur.com/article/243589

Wood, J. (n.d.). Working from home? Here's how to stay on task. https://wavelength.asana.com/workstyle-working-from-home-heres-how-to-stay-on-task/

Acknowledgements

My gratitude and thanks for support over the years to:

My Parents and in-laws, my sister Jade and my own family, Nicola, Ben, and Lily.

Thomas Edwards, John Knapp and Kevin Munson as mentors through my working career.

Dr. Andrew Gould PhD, my mentor and friend through my academic studies.

Christian and Rasmus, for opening my mind to actually making this book a reality.

Printed by Amazon Italia Logistica S.r.l.
Torrazza Piemonte (TO), Italy